Everyday Ways to Raise Smart, Strong, Confident Girls

Also by Barbara Littman

The Women's Business Resource Guide

Everyday Ways to Raise Smart, Strong, Confident Girls

Successful Teens Tell Us What Works

Barbara Littman

Thomas Dunne Books
St. Martin's Griffin ✤ New York

THOMAS DUNNE BOOKS.
An imprint of St. Martin's Press.

Book design by Ellen R. Sasahara

Library of Congress Cataloging-in-Publication Data

Littman, Barbara
    Everyday ways to raise smart, strong, confident girls : successful
teens tell us what works / Barbara Littman.
        p.   cm.
    Includes bibliographical references and index.
    ISBN 0-312-20973-8
1. Teenage girls—United States.   2. Self-esteem in adolescence—
United States.   3. Self-confidence.   4. Parent and teenager—
United States.   5. Teenage girls—United States Bibliography.
6. Teenage girls—Services for—United States Directories.
I. Title.
HQ798.L57   1999   99-31472
649'.133—dc21   CIP

First St. Martin's Griffin Edition: September 1999

10 9 8 7 6 5 4 3 2 1

Contents

Preface

When I was growing up in the sixties and seventies, the women's movement held out great promise and hope for young women who wanted to pursue dreams and goals outside the home.

And in more ways than we can count, it delivered on that promise. Harassment, sexism, unequal pay, and other gender-based discrimination still exist, but it's fair to say 'we've made great progress.'

Assumed, but not realized, was the tacit belief that future generations of girls would benefit from the work of second-wave feminism. And while they have—with increased career and educational opportunities, more life choices, and improved health care that acknowledges women's unique needs—girls are still struggling. Their self-esteem, health, and optimism continue to suffer:

- In elementary school, 45 percent of girls say they are "good at lots of things." In middle school the percentage drops to 29 percent and in high school to 23 percent. (Boys start at 55 percent and drop to 42 percent by high school.)
- In elementary school, 60 percent of girls say they are "happy with the way I am." In middle school the percentage drops to 37 percent and in high school to 29 percent. (Boys start at 67 percent and drop to 46 percent by high school.)
- Each year in the United States, approximately 1 million teenage girls become pregnant, and over half of them carry their babies to term.
- Nearly 10 percent of teen girls suffer from anorexia, and it's estimated that 6 percent of all anorexics die from the disease.

• Teenage girls consider and attempt suicide more frequently than boys. In one study, nearly twice as many ninth-grade girls as boys considered suicide (34 percent of girls versus 18 percent of boys), and twice as many girls made an attempt (15 percent versus 7 percent).

Mary Pipher, in her groundbreaking book *Reviving Ophelia: Saving the Selves of Adolescent Girls,* could not have put it better: "Just as planes and ships disappear mysteriously in the Bermuda Triangle, so do the selves of girls go down in droves."

Yet, there are girls who are thriving, and it was in meeting and working with one of these girls that the idea for this book first took root. Blair Saxon-Hill, who later became a member of my teen advisory board for this book, applied for a job to help me develop part of a Web site for my local school district. I hired several boys and her. Her thoughtfulness and insight were immediately apparent, and as I got to know her better, I became intrigued by how she had managed to preserve her self-esteem and enthusiasm when so many girls her age do not.

As I became more serious about writing a book about teen girls who are thriving against the odds, she helped me organize a teen advisory board. The board was made up of a remarkable collection of thoughtful, articulate, involved young women. It included activists, a writer, a musician, an athlete, and an artist. I had regular meetings with this group over a four-month period, during which their openness and ideas guided me in the development of the book.

The question that emerged from my meetings with them was simple: What experiences have these girls, and others like them, had that contributed to their self-esteem and ability to remain involved and optimistic during a period when girls so often drop out of constructive activities?

My conversations with my advisory board told me in no uncertain terms that these girls had many of the answers. Why not ask them? And so I did, in a ten-question survey that was completed by eighty-one girls from around the country. (My survey questions can be found on p. 000.) The girls were hand-picked by adults who knew them and knew they were beating the odds: Survey respondents were selected because they were successful in school, did not abuse drugs, and were involved in and enthusiastic about a variety of activities. Most of the girls selected were between the ages of sixteen and twenty and represented a cross-section of the population. (Survey respondents included thirty African-Americans, twenty-nine Caucasians, thirteen Hispanics, five Asian-Americans, one "multi-cultural," and three who declined to answer the question about their ethnic or racial affiliation. One of these girls wrote, "I'm human and my race is not going to affect my ability to achieve my dreams." It was an answer that pleased me.)

After all the surveys were returned and I began to review girls' responses, I organized another small group of girls to serve as my editorial board. (My advisory board members were far-flung by then, most scattered around the country attending college.) Another remarkable group, these young women provided me with insights that helped me better understand the varied and thoughtful responses on the surveys.

This book was really written by the girls who gave their time and thoughtfulness to this project. We—parents, teachers, and other adults who want to help girls flourish—have much to gain by listening to them and trying the things they say have worked for them.

Acknowledgments

This book would not have been possible without the help and interest of many people and organizations.

First, I want to thank all the girls and young women whose ideas are included. First and foremost, I want to thank my teen advisory board and editorial board members, whose interest, honesty, time, and good ideas allowed me see the world from their perspective and offer their insights to adults who want to help girls flourish: Megan Chinburg, Talya Husbands-Hankins, Amy Isham, Katie Humphrey, Gabrielle Lerner, Hilary Neevel, Stefanie Rimel, Blair Saxon-Hill, Kate Skillman, and Megan Thompson.

Second, I want to thank all the girls who took time to complete my survey and whose thoughtfulness and good ideas made the book possible:

Megan Ablott	Brandy Fargon
Francine Alvarado	Maria Garcia
Veronica Isabel Aquilar	Hilda Daniela Gonzalez
Aasha Artis	Luri Gonzalez
Lilah Baker-Rabe	Angela Rose Guidry
Crystal Bell	Alayna Haberlin
Kristen Benge	Sheronne Harrell
Susie Pauline Benniefield	Kia Haselrig
Jennifer Blockburger	Sarah Hodges
Marneissa Brown	Tiffany Howard
Jamie Diane Carter	Rozmond Collins Johnson
Kathleen Cassard	Tiffany Jones
Christa Dow	Angela Kalanick

Megan Kin
Darlene Lebron
Donniese Lemmon
Geneva Lightfoot
Christine Long
Audrey Lopez
Michelle Mantegani
Sarah McGettigan
Tahita McHenry
Kaletta Mennis
Cosina Nashea Morrison
Genevieve R. Nolte
Cynthia Padilla
Alisha Palmer
Tavonna Payne
Gabriela Perez
Valentina Pinedo
La Tania Nicole Pitts
Margaret Pizzitola
Chely Rodriguez

Marisol Sanchez
Alisha Shelton
Angela Sidenar
Nihesha Simmons
Marlisha Smith
Shamura Smith
Jessica Steen
Stephanie Stevens
Kim Thi My Le
Rashelle Thomas
Carolyn Tobias
Mian Tran
Jessica Turner
Loan Vo
Yovanda Walls
Lezlie Watson
Sarah Wesley
Juliet Wong
Marcelle Young

Note: Of the eighty-one girls who completed the survey, thirteen asked to remain anonymous. In addition to the list of sixty-five girls above and the thirteen anonymous girls, three of my advisory board members also completed a survey. (All of my advisory board members are listed in the first paragraph of the acknowledgments.)

Thank you also to the organizations and their staff members who helped recruit girls to complete the survey:

American Association of
    University Women
An Income of Her Own
National Association for Girls
    & Women in Sport
Daughters Newsletter
Denver Kids
Girls' Choir of Harlem

Girls Count
Girls Incorporated
Girl Scouts of the USA
Girls Speak Out
I Have A Dream Foundation
New Moon Publishing
Mi Casa Resource Center for
    Women

Mission Bay High School   St. Agnes Academy
Mt. Vernon High School   St. Mary's Academy

Thank you also to my agent, Denise Marcil, whose interest and guidance made this book possible, and to my editor, Melissa Jacobs, whose enthusiasm and critical eye helped shape the book's final form.

Family First

Family is the first topic girls bring up when asked about aspects of their lives that help them resist or overcome a drop in self-esteem. For many girls their home is the first—and sometimes only—place they feel important, valued, and appreciated. The sense of self they develop as a result gives them a confidence and resilience they perceive as lacking in girls around them who are more easily influenced by their peers and the media.

Doing things together is a critical aspect of guiding girls toward self-esteem, and confidence, but it alone is not enough. Girls are as sensitive to *how* you do things together as they are to *what* you do together. As a result, some of the ideas in this chapter are about parents' behavior. Girls also like to do different things with their mothers and with fathers, so these ideas are included in the "Special Advice for Dads," and "Special Advice for Mothers" sections.

1. Eat Meals Together

This has be the number-one event girls mentioned that made them feel good about themselves in the family setting, and it carries over to other areas of their lives.

Even if it happens less often than in previous generations, girls value having meals with their families. From meals at home with the whole family to weekly dinners at "grandma's" to fast-food dinners when no one has time to cook to sharing infrequent special meals like Thanksgiving, sitting down at the same time in the same place to eat is at the top of girls' lists.

But eating together is not enough. It's the conversation and op-

1

portunity to learn about each other that are important. This is a great time to listen to your daughter and to try to understand her world. Girls often feel small and ignored in our fast-paced world. They need to know they count, and meals are a great time to let them know they do.

Meals with an extended family on a regular basis also get high marks from girls as a time when they can hang out with family members. Conversation, food preparation, and caring for the younger kids all provide a sense of belonging and comfort girls are looking for.

"We discuss what we did during the week. Even if it ends up in an argument, we apologize and show each other we care. If everyone just sits down together, a lot of problems can be prevented!"
—15-year-old survey respondent

"The fact that my parents and siblings wanted to be a part of the activity really made me feel that my conversation, news, and ideas could be validated by people I care about and who care about me."
—15-year-old survey respondent

> If you have trouble talking with your daughter or want to open the channels of communication, check out *How to Talk So Kids Will Listen and Listen So Kids Will Talk, Talking So Teens Listen,* and *Parent-Teen Breakthrough: The Relationship Approach* for ideas about how you and your daughter can have meaningful conversations without fighting. These books are described in the list of "Books and Newsletters for Adults" that starts on page 133.

2. Build a Community of Caring Adults

Bring many adults into your daughter's sphere. The key is that the adults (parents included) engage the girl in interesting, meaningful conversations, encourage her to speak up, and value and respect her ideas and opinions. Girls talk about being strongly influenced by adults (other than their parents) who participate in family activities. And dinner is a time girls especially enjoy when there is a group of interested and interesting adults talking, laughing, asking questions, and listening.

One girl spoke fondly of watching her mother hold up a friend's new baby at the dinner table to be cooed at and admired by everyone. She knew the same had been done for her when she was growing up, and that that small event marked the beginning of her initiation into a group of caring adults.

"The most important thing in my family is that I spend time around adults who take me seriously."
—17-year-old advisory board member

3. Tell on Yourself

Girls are hungry to know who their parents are, warts and all; the perfect parent is intimidating. Girls don't feel perfect, and they want to know that imperfection is normal.

One girl described her love for and feelings of connection to her father when he talked about a traumatic incident that occurred when he was a young adult: he had accidentally caused a serious injury to a co-worker by being careless. Hearing this story and others like it told the girl her father trusted her. That trust has allowed her to reveal things to her father about herself that many teens hide from parents.

One of the most popular kinds of columns in girls' magazines is the "true nightmare" story. Misery does love company! Tell on yourself over and over again. It's a great way to keep the lines of communication open and establish trust and empathy with your daughter.

The columns go by different names—everything from "Holy Guacamole!" in *Girls' Life* to "Trauma-rama" in *Seventeen*. Read a few and get a picture of what girls find mortifying.

"I remember when my mother told me about how scared she was on her first date—who the boy was and how crazy she was about him—I

3

*couldn't stop laughing. Just before my first date, I told her I was really
nervous. And then we both couldn't stop laughing.*"
—18-year-old survey respondent

4. Tell Stories About Your Life

In addition to learning about adults' bad moments, daughters also
want information about important events and people in their parents' lives. Girls want to know how their parents met. Was it love
at first sight? What was the first house or apartment like that you
lived in after getting married? What was your first job out of high
school or college? Who was the best teacher you ever had? Who was
the worst?

Try not to use the stories to lecture or make a moral point. Just
tell stories! Let them reveal something about yourself. Use them to
become a real person to your daughter so she has a sense of who you
are and what you care about.

Girls who get to know their parents in this way see them as
people, not just parents, and they reciprocate with stories about
themselves.

*"My mother sits and tells me stories of how she was when she was my
age and my grandmother did the same for her. Taking much learning
from my grandmother, my mother is a strong woman who has influenced
me to be the same."*
—17-year-old survey respondent

5. Hold Family Gatherings

Girls say they like reunions because it helps them feel like they are
a part of a group that cares about them. Reunions are a time when
daughters get to learn about where you came from, and meet and
talk to people who made a difference in your life when you were
young. And, of course, they get to hear stories about you. Many of
the silly, embarrassing tales that emerge in these settings help your
daughter understand and appreciate you. She will see that you really
are human and went through a lot of the same confusing, embarrassing, and exciting moments she experiences!

If you don't have a family, your family is too far-flung for reunions, or you are not close to your family, consider developing a surrogate family of loving friends or draw from your community of caring adults. This family-like group can fulfill girls' desire to belong, as well as provide opportunities to do fun, interesting things with different people. In addition, girls can turn to individual members of the group for special guidance. Sometimes a daughter might not feel comfortable talking with her parents about something but wants to discuss a problem with an adult she knows and trusts. Whether she chooses your best friend, her best friend's mother, or another caring adult, these can be the people who provide what grandmothers and aunts might in a close-knit family.

"Family reunions helped build my self-esteem because I knew my family would always be there for me when I needed them, and I know that wherever I go I will always have a loving and forgiving family."
—15-year-old survey respondent

"When we are all together, I feel special. We laugh and talk about how everyone is doing. One thing I like most is when my mother boasts about me. I like to see her smile and talk about how well I am doing."
—16-year-old survey respondent

"Every year my family drives to reunite with other family members. This activity contributes to my self-esteem because whenever I feel discouraged, there is someone to kindle my spirits. The one who really keeps the family together is my grandmother. She leads everyone in the right direction and will not settle for anything less."
—17-year-old survey respondent

6. Take Trips Together

Girls described family trips as "adventures" they really enjoy, especially when they are involved in planning where the family goes and in the trip preparation. If you don't like the idea of finding out that someone bigger and older than you has decided when and where you're going to spend your two-week annual vacation, it doesn't take much to figure out that girls don't like it either. It's hard to have fun and feel good about the people you're with when you don't want to be where you are—even harder if you feel like no one cares that you don't want to be there. Most families take vacations and trips together, but they're often not a lot of fun. When teens are resentful followers, it can ruin a vacation. Planning together may mean some compromise for everyone, but when your daughter is involved in choosing and planning the vacation because it's her fun on the line too she has an added incentive!

When a tight budget needs to be followed before or during the trip, let your daughter in on the secret. Girls like this kind of involvement and don't see it as a hardship when everyone is in it together.

Continue to involve your daughter in decisions once you set out on the trip. Remember, as important as getting where you need to go is the message you send her about her importance and role in the family. Where will you eat? How long will you stay? Let her help with these decisions so she feels influential and recognizes that she has good ideas to contribute.

"The trip we go on every summer is traditional. My aunt is like a mother to me on the trips and we spend a lot of time together talking. It makes me feel so good."
—15-year-old survey respondent

"My family always used to go to Yosemite before Christmas. The time we spent there really brought us together. It was something constant that I could depend on and it helped me gain confidence through stability."
—16-year-old survey respondent

7. Involve Her in Shared Decision-Making

If you want a self-reliant, thoughtful teen, include her in the decision-making process for events that affect her life. While parents who use shared decision-making see increased cooperation from their daughters as a major benefit, daughters see the benefits differently. Of most importance to them is having a place in their lives where what they say matters and what they want has an influence on the final outcome. Knowing that what they want and what they say at home matters helps them in other areas of their lives. They are more confident about speaking out at school and with peers.

6

"My parents don't always get what they want this way, but they know they're getting something more important. Sometimes my sister and I just go along with what my parents want because we know it's important to them. It makes us feel good to do that because they're so fair."
—17-year-old advisory board member

"I think her [mother] asking me for my opinions and ideas and reaffirming them really made a difference in the way I view my own thoughts."
—15-year-old survey respondent

In the 1996 report *Girls in the Middle: Working to Succeed in School* from the American Association of University Women (AAUW), "speaking out" was identified as one of the strategies girls use to achieve success in school. (See page 175 for more information about the AAUW and its reports.)

8. Hold Family Meetings

One girl called it "quality time," another "family meeting night," but the purpose of the activity is the same: a time set aside when family members can bring up things on their minds. It's a time for your daughter to explain why she doesn't think your curfew is fair, or how she felt when you said you would be at the game but didn't show, or to tell you she really appreciates the time you spent volunteering with her group.

You get a turn too. And as the adult and role model, it's important that you are constructive, nonjudgmental, and positive. Make the time fun, but serious. It's not that different from a meeting at work or a service group when people come together to go over what's been accomplished, what needs to be done next, and how things can be improved.

Just as with family dinners, these sessions can offer a girl one of the few times when she is listened to and respected. If she is going to speak up in the "real" world, these family meetings can be her practice field. One girl whose family started these kinds of meetings

7

when she was young said she thought they were "dumb" at the time, but came to appreciate how much they helped her in later years.

"Growing up in my family, we had a thing called quality time when everyone gets together and discusses what has happened to them or family business that needs to be mentioned. It helped me get used to talking to people even if it was my family members."
—17-year-old survey respondent

9. Go Camping

Girls said camping is different from a "trip." On a trip, there are lots of things to do and plan; camping is a time when hanging out is the main thing to do and girls enjoy the undivided attention they get from their parents. No one has to deal with the daily pressures of everyday life or the realities of taking a trip, like finding and checking into motels, deciding where to go for dinner, or getting to an event on time. And camping, unlike urban vacations, offers opportunities to enjoy nature together and instill in your daughter a love of the outdoors and an appreciation of the natural environment.

For families who don't like to camp, or can't, consider an occasional vacation where most of your daily needs are met and you can just spend time hanging out with your daughter.

Girls talk about wanting to have (and enjoying) their parents' undivided attention in lots of other situations too, like playing sports together. So if you can't camp, keep in mind that camping, while fun, is the means to an end for girls: being the focus of attention in their parents' lives. Look for alternatives to camping that provide for most of your needs so you can have some undivided time with your daughter.

"Camping was just me and my family. No need to rush, wake up, or do something. It was a time for a few weeks each summer when I didn't have to do battle for my parents' attention."
—18-year-old survey respondent

"My family has, for as long as I can remember, taken vacations together in the summer. These vacations were always backpacking trips some-

where in the wilderness. Because we were isolated from everything else, we spent all of our vacation time together."
—18-year-old advisory board member

10. Don't Put Your Daughter Down in Front of Other People

Girls say they want to cringe when they hear parents criticize their child in front of other people. One girl observed many of her friends' parents making mean or undermining comments about their children, and made an agreement with her mother that neither one of them would ever make derogatory or critical comments about each other in public.

Girls who have seen their friends put down in front of others, or who have been the target of comments themselves, describe the experience as "soul-withering." Public humiliation is painful for everyone. For a tender new self, it can be annihilating.

> Unsupportive criticism and undermining comments never feel good, but teenage girls may be especially vulnerable to their effects; they are twice as likely as boys to become depressed during adolescence, with depression rates as high as 30 percent.

"Embarrassing her, putting her down in front of friends, or bad-mouthing her is horrible. It embarrasses me when a parent does that to her daughter in front of me. I instantly lose respect for any parent that does that to their child."
—18-year-old advisory board member

11. Don't Push

When someone pushes, most people push back. For teens, this natural inclination to push back easily becomes rebellion. Girls talk about how quickly and easily they resist their parents when they feel they are being pushed or manipulated into doing something. (Practicing the shared decision-making described in Activity No. 7 will foster cooperation.)

Girls say that when they hear comments like "Because I said so" and "I'm you're father," they can feel their heels digging in. And the harder the push, the deeper the digging.

> For tips on how to have reasonable discussions with your teenager, again I recommend reading the perennially popular *How to Talk So Kids Will Listen and Listen So Kids Will Talk* (page 136).

"My parents are really reasonable. I mean it makes a difference what I say, but I have friends who lie to their parents all the time just so they won't end up in a fight."
— 18-year-old advisory board member

12. Attend Church Together

When girls talk about attending church, they don't mention the religious experience as much as they do the social one: feeling close to family members, singing, attending church dinners, participating in the youth group, and looking up to an adult member of their church are all key activities they say bring them self-esteem and confidence.

(Many of the survey respondents were Christian, so "church" was specifically mentioned, but it is hard to believe the same would not hold true for girls' experiences attending other houses of worship with their families.)

If you aren't religious or don't attend an organized church, consider becoming involved in a cultural or ethnic group where your daughter can find a similar sense of belonging to a group your family is committed to.

"Singing in church with my grandparents contributed greatly to my self-esteem. Getting together with other people, making music, and sharing time with my grandparents made me feel alive. I felt like I belonged somewhere and that I was being encouraged to use a part of me (my voice) to create something positive."
— 20-year-old survey respondent

10

"I went to Paris and Rome with my youth group for 'World Youth Day.' I can't even put into words how amazing this trip was. My youth group has helped me stay positive and keep away from negative things like drugs and alcohol. I've met so many wonderful people who continue to be positive influences in my life."
—16-year-old survey respondent

"Encourage girls to research their cultural heritage. Provide resources!"
—20-year-old survey respondent

13. Read Together and Provide Her with Meaningful Books

One survey respondent who loves to read could not have put it better: "Encourage your daughter to read books that feed her heart and mind."

You can feed her heart and mind by introducing her to books that will help her feel good about herself and about being female. Books that speak to the issues girls confront as they move from their pre-teen years to adolescence and young womanhood let her know she is not alone. And books about strong girls and women can open windows of possibility and inspire your daughter to dream big and believe she can achieve her dreams.

There are lots of books to comfort, inspire, and empower. Check out the list of "Books for Girls" on page 125 and the list of "Books about Good Books for Girls" on page 130 for help selecting additional good reading for your daughter. Also, check the lists for specific resource topics, like "Sports and Physical Fitness" and "Math, Science, and Technology," for more books to educate and inspire girls who have expressed interest in a specific area.

Reading together is a way to use books to feed your daughter's heart and mind, and it can provide a basis for shared experience and discussion. Sometimes girls who cannot identify issues or are afraid to speak about their own fears and dreams can do so by referring to a fictional character or role model in a biography.

One girl who enjoys reading and discussing books with her mother discovered an added benefit of sharing their love of reading. The process of going to the bookstore, discussing the different titles before making a purchase, and going for coffee afterward made it easier to bring up other topics.

For guidance in how to share reading with your daughter, take a look at *The Mother-Daughter Book Club: How Ten Busy Mothers and Daughters Came Together to Talk, Laugh, and Learn Through Their Love of Reading* (page 132). This book describes a great program for mothers who want to start a reading group with other mothers and their daughters.

"The intimate setting of a bookstore on Saturday afternoon engenders honesty and openness in our conversations."
—18-year-old advisory board member

"Reading Gloria Steinem's Revolution from Within *changed my thinking forever. And going to a 'Riot Grrrl' convention was a powerful and positive experience."*
—20-year-old survey respondent

14. Teach Your Daughters to Cook and Do Basic Maintenance

While girls often identify the mother as the "cooking teacher" and the father as the "maintenance teacher," responses to the survey show this isn't always the case. It doesn't seem to matter who teaches girls these skills; they want them in order to be independent.

Girls who did not have cooking and maintenance skills made this suggestion after realizing that, once on their own, there were lots of things they had taken for granted. They discovered they didn't know how to handle some important areas of their lives.

Girls who went out on their own after high school, to start either college or work, wanted to know how to fix a flat tire or a leaky faucet and how to cook good food so their budgets and diets were reasonable.

Whether your family responsibilities are divided along traditional gender lines or not, include your daughter in life-skill activities, from cooking and car maintenance to money management. (For lots of girls' good ideas about encouraging money management, see "What Can She Be?" starting on page 87.) For single moms or women who don't want to rely on a spouse or man for traditionally male tasks, consider taking home- and car-maintenance classes with your daughter at a local community college. If you're a dad (or mom) who's a klutz in the kitchen, a cooking class with your daughter can be a fun way to learn together and get in a little bit of good eating at the same time.

"Fathers should encourage girls to do 'male' activities too, like mowing the grass, fixing a leaky faucet, or changing the oil in the car. It helps them bond and it's also important to learn how to do chores that once belonged to men because it makes us less dependent on others and more confident, capable beings."
—20-year-old survey respondent

15. Establish a Let's Play Hooky Day

Girls feel many of the same stresses in life that adults do. They worry about playing well in an upcoming sports event, how they look, homework deadlines, and how they did on their last test. Girls say they like to take a day off when they're supposed to be in school and do something fun with their families.

Plan a day off for yourself and do something relaxing with your daughter. Some of the things girls like to do on a hooky day are:

- Leave town for a short day trip.
- Go shopping for new clothes and then go out to lunch.
- Visit a museum and then take a walk.

- Plan a great meal, shop for everything you need to prepare it, and then put on some favorite music while you cook.

Hooky days don't need to be elaborate. In fact, if they become elaborate, they don't count. There shouldn't have to be much planning and preparation.

"My parents took my sister and me out of school a couple of times a year to do something fun. I remember I felt so special on those days, like I was getting to do something no one else in the whole world got to do."
—19-year-old survey respondent

16. Use Personality Profiles to Build Acceptance and Appreciation

When teens hit high school, they are often required to take personality and preference tests to help them explore career and work choices.

One of these preference tests, the Meyers-Briggs Type Indicator, is helpful in the family setting. Girls who take the test in school and then bring it home for the family to take report improved relationships with their parents and other family members.

The beauty of the Meyers-Briggs is that its purpose is not to categorize people, but rather to help them understand and appreciate themselves and each other. Based on your answers to over fifty questions, the test rates you on eight characteristics (for example, whether you tend toward being introverted or extroverted) and then assigns a profile type. Girls say they enjoy getting the results because it helps them like themselves better and understand why they do things that seem out of step with other people sometimes. In addition, it helps them understand their friends who have also taken the test in school.

One girl said she figured out what type her parents were before she asked them to take the test. Before they even had an opportunity to take the test and talk over the results, she felt better about some of the things they did that she previously found confusing. Thinking about the test helped her understand that her parents are not just parents; they are people, with their own quirks and styles.

Once you know your own and each others' types, don't stop there. Post them and the characteristics on the refrigerator. When a disagreement or misunderstanding comes up, check back to the fridge. The differences between types will give you clues about what is going wrong in your conversation. Type tracking can also be fun source of affectionate teasing.

For a book with a self-scoring test based on the Meyers-Briggs and a good discussion of the implications types have in the family setting, read *Please Understand Me II* (David Keirsey and Marilyn Bates, Prometheus Nemesis Books). You can also visit the publisher's Web site at http://keirsey.com and take a test right on-line.

"My mother and I are a lot alike and really different from my father. Now [since taking the Meyers-Briggs] we understand him better. We can actually tease him about how logical he is and no one gets upset."
—18-year-old advisory board member

17. Laugh Together

Some people say the family that prays together, stays together. If teen girls were writing the rules, they would say the family that laughs together, stays together.

Watching funny videos and movies together and reading funny books and silly joke books are all ways girls keep laughing with their parents. One girl said whenever the family travels, they take along a silly joke book and take turns reading from it. Girls need to laugh. At an age when self-doubt and depression strike so many, laughter can be a light at the end of the tunnel.

Girls especially like humor about women and men. Even with their limited experience with boys, gender humor hits home. Books that take a light-hearted look at the battle of the sexes appeal to girls. A favorite in this genre is *Why Dogs Are Better than Men* (Jennifer Berman, Pocket Books).

Some great books to keep around the house and in the car include *1000 Jokes for Kids of All Ages* (Michael Kilgarriff, Ballantine), *500 Hilarious Jokes for Kids* (Jeff Rovin, New American Library), *101 Back to School Jokes* (Lisa Eisenberg and Katy Hall, Scholastic), *101 Hopelessly Hilarious Jokes* (Lisa Eisenberg and Katy Hall, Scholastic), and *Laughing Together* (Barbara Walker, Free Spirit).

Another important way to keep laughing with your daughter is to keep your own sense of humor through the difficulties of raising a teen. Fortunately, there are lots of books available to help you do just that. Take a look at *Get Out of My Life: But First Could You Drive Me and Cheryl to the Mall?* (Anthony Wolf, Noonday Press), *Rebel Without a Car: Surviving and Appreciating Your Child's Teen Years* (Fred Mednick, Fairview Press), and *Power Parenting Your Teenager* (Mary Eve Corbel, Hysteria Publications).

18. Establish Rituals and Celebrations

Girls say it's easy for them to feel invisible. At school they see boys receive more attention than they do for both good and bad behavior. They see women treated as sexual objects in the media, receiving recognition not for what they do, but for how they look.

To get a thought-provoking picture of just how invisible girls can be in school and still get by, see *Failing at Fairness: How Our Schools Cheat Girls* (page 166).To understand better how women are portrayed in demeaning and unrealistic ways, check out the Web sites and publications in the "Body Image and Media Representation of Women" listing page 140.

Girls want to be recognized and appreciated for their accomplishments and abilities, and rituals and celebrations can help them do this. One Jewish girl described how fortunate she felt to have a built-in rite of passage in the bat mitzvah celebration.

Don't let your daughters' accomplishments go unnoticed, no

matter how big or small. When your daughter reaches a goal or does well in an important activity, celebrate. Give her a card of congratulations, or take her out for dinner.

Celebrate each of her birthdays in a special way that recognizes her new capabilities. One girl described how her parents kept a photo album dedicated to her, and on each of her birthdays added pictures taken the previous year showing her as a strong and interesting girl.

For some ideas and tips about how to recognize your daughter for being female *and* for her accomplishments, take a look at *Celebrating Girls: Nurturing and Empowering Our Daughters.* The newsletter *New Moon Network* also often has articles about how to recognize girls' accomplishments and celebrate their passages. For more information about these two resources, see the list of "Books and Newsletters for Adults" on page 133. *Rituals for Our Times: Celebrating, Healing and Changing Our Lives and Relationships* (Evan Imber-Blackand and Janice Roberts, HarperCollins), though not about girls or children specifically, is another great resource for parents who want to understand the importance of rituals and how to incorporate them into their family life.

19. Treat Boys and Girls Equally

When girls talk about this subject, they're talking about encouragement and opportunity. They recognize that girls and boys (and men and women!) are not the same. They also recognize that there are some legitimate times when girls and boys cannot be treated the same, like in situations where girls may be at risk for sexual assault.

But in general, they want to have the same opportunities and receive the same encouragement as boys. Yes, they can be athletes and scientists, participate in physically challenging activities, fix up an old car or start a Web page design business.

When girls get the message at home from an early age that they can participate fully in the same kinds of activities boys do, it is easier for them to ignore or resist messages that pigeonhole girls and women in traditional roles.

"Something really important is that my parents did the same activities with me that they did with my brother. My parents never gave me the feeling that I was capable of anything less than my brother."
—18-year-old advisory board member

"Instill girls with the knowledge of equality. This lesson is crucial to everyone, but for a girl to understand her equality with boys and still treasure her uniqueness could have a profoundly positive effect on her outlook."
—20-year-old survey respondent

20. Don't Try to Be Your Daughter's Pal

Girls want to like and trust their parents, but they don't want to be pals. They want to know that their parents are older and more mature than they are so they have someone to count on when they need help or advice.

Girls described parental relationships that were "too close" in different ways. Fathers who were too close were described as interfering and overbearing, and mothers who tried to be their daughter's pal were seen as suffocating.

Girls said it was easier to have pal-like relationships with their fathers than with their mothers, because time with fathers usually involved doing something. When a mother is too close, or a best friend, it is not a friendship of equals. And while they do want to know what their mothers think and feel, they may not feel equipped to hear about deep problems. They know who the adult is, and they want the adult to know it too.

All of this does not mean girls don't want their parents to be friends. In fact they often say they would like their parents to be "a friend, not just a parent." This distinction is qualified with a description of a "parental friend" as someone who listens, provides support, and acts as an adviser. Girls don't want a parent to tell them "what to do and what not to do." They want a parent who will help them figure out how to handle life's ups and downs.

"I definitely do not want my parents trying to be a teenager with me!"
—17-year-old advisory board member

"Guide your daughter in the right direction. Don't tell her what to do. Instead show her what she can be heading for."
—19-year-old survey respondent

21. Respect Her Privacy

As girls hit adolescence they begin to separate from their parents as a natural part of growing up. Ironically, it's also a time when parents—very legitimately—have concerns about their daughters' safety as they venture out more on their own.

Balancing your desire to know all the details with your daughter's right for privacy—and the respect implied when you acknowledge that right—is a tricky feat to accomplish. But, according to girls, it is a balancing act that is well worth the effort. Nosy parents drive girls underground, exactly the opposite result parents want. Think about what privacy means in your own life. Think about what it means for a young girl at a stage when new feelings and experiences are a daily occurrence.

What does privacy mean for girls? They describe it as "psychological and physical space." They want to have private conversations with friends that their parents can't overhear. They may be talking about perfectly innocent topics, but they still want their privacy. They want a room that is their own, kept as tidy or messy as they want it to be. And keeping the door closed is fine with them. Parents don't have to look at it, and girls don't have to hear parental complaints. Diaries and journals are a place where girls work out things in their lives, not a place where they have to monitor what they write because they are afraid a parent will read it.

For some interesting insights into what girls' bedrooms mean to them during the early teen years, take a look at *The Roller Coaster Years: Raising Your Child Through the Maddening Yet Magical Middle-School Years* (see the "Books and Newsletters for Adults" resource lisitings on page 133 for more information).

Girls who share their lives with their parents say it's because their parents share their lives with them. If you're telling stories on yourself, telling stories about your life, and involving your daughter in shared decision-making (Activities Nos. 3, 4, and 7), odds are high you're creating a climate in which your daughter will share her life with you. Maybe not every detail (because she still will want some separation and privacy), but the important stuff. And if you're concerned about something, girls have some refreshing advice: Ask!

"When I was in middle school, I didn't even want my mom to hear me on the phone with my friends. I wasn't talking about anything bad, I just didn't want her to hear. When I look back on it now, it seems really stupid, but at the time it was really important to me that there were just some things my mom wasn't involved in."
—18-year-old editorial board member

"I am very close to my mother. We talk about a lot of things, but some things I just don't want to talk with her about. I know it's hard for her, but she respects it and I really appreciate that."
—16-year-old survey respondent

22. Don't Be Afraid to Talk About Sex

Girls often get a lot of information from parents or school about the physiological changes their bodies are going through. But they also want to know the facts about pregnancy, AIDS, and other sexually transmitted diseases, contraception, how sex relates to love, relationships, and other sexuality issues.

Be aware, though, that limited access to information on these topics can be dangerous. While the United States has the highest teen-pregnancy rate in the industrialized nations, the nineties saw a decline in this country. This decline followed active educational efforts in the late 1980s, indicating that teen behavior *can* be influenced by information and resources.

Parents can use this knowledge that information about sexuality, pregnancy, disease, and related topics can have a positive effect on their daughter's behavior. Study these topics with her and talk about the implications for her. In your discussions, address the contradictory messages she receives about the meaning of sex: it can be dangerous for girls, yet being sexy significantly defines women's perceived value in our culture. There are lots of places to go for information. Check out Sexuality Information and Education Council of the U.S. (SIECUS) and Advocates for Youth and Planned Parenthood. SIECUS and Advocates have publications and programs about sexuality issues, and the SIECUS Web site includes an extensive reading list for parents and teens. The Planned Parenthood Web site has on-line guides for parents on topics such as talking about sex and birth control, as well as information for teens. (All these organizations are described in the "Staying Safe and In Control" resource listings on page 188.) Mothers who want guidance about how to discuss sex with their daughters can get lots of good advice from *Venus in Blue Jeans: Why Mothers and Daughters Need to Talk About Sex,* described on page 191.

Research conducted by the U.S. Department of Health and Human Services found that teen participation in sex-education programs did not increase their sexual activity, and teens who participated in abstinence-only education did not reduce sexual activity.

Consider also the possibility that your daughter may be a lesbian, or bisexual. This will not mean different facts about how her body changes at puberty, but it will mean different kinds of feelings for both of you.

Organizations like Parents, Families and Friends of Gays and Lesbians (see page 123) can help on this issue. Request information about their booklets *Be Yourself* (for teens) and *Our Daughters and Sons* (for parents). Both include questions and answers, background information, and resource listings of helpful books, magazines, and other organizations.

"Don't be afraid to discuss sex and sexuality. They are embarrassing issues for girls to deal with but I learned more from my mom than from my friends. Adults know more about it than we do!"
   —18-year-old survey respondent

21

SPECIAL ADVICE FOR DADS

23. Dad, Do Something with Your Daughter

Girls say they often feel their fathers distancing themselves as the change from girl to young woman occurs. They sense their father's dismay and discomfort at the changes their bodies are going through, and they miss the easy comfort of hanging out with Dad.

Girls say unequivocally that this distancing has an effect on how they feel in their relationships with boys. While it may be inevitable to some degree, it is their first little taste of betrayal by the opposite sex—and, worst of all, for something they have absolutely no control over.

As your daughter moves into adolescence, keep doing things with her. If you shot hoops, went for bike rides, or trained the dog together when she was young, keep doing it. If you're good at something she shows an interest in, from business to sports and anything in between, invite her to participate.

Girls who share an important activity with their fathers say it makes them feel important in his eyes and directly affects their self-esteem and confidence. Do something together every week. Go to a movie and then talk about it afterwards. Attend sports events together or shop for a present for a sibling or friend. The key is to stay connected and in touch so trust and communication continue.

"My father sings and plays the guitar and we have a special song we sing together. At his fiftieth birthday party he invited me up on stage to sing our song in front of close friends and the family. I felt proud to be his daughter and I'm sure he felt proud to be my dad."
    —18-year-old survey respondent

"My dad likes to work on old cars and he never told me that I couldn't help, even when I was younger. I passed him tools and watched and learned. We had lots of quality time together and I really enjoyed it."
    —18-year-old respondent

24. Treat the Women in Your Life Well

Your daughter is watching how you treat women and girls. This means your wife or girlfriend, your daughter's friends, work associates, a friend, a neighbor, or any other women you have contact with, even if briefly over a cash register.

Think about how you want your daughter to be treated by the men and boys she is close to and by men with whom she may have passing contact. If you want her to be treated respectfully, be encouraged to speak her mind, and feel safe physically and psychologically, then treat the women in your life that way. When you treat the women around you respectfully you are building your daughter's mental model of acceptable and desirable male behavior.

Girls who grow up abused or observing abuse often expect to be treated abusively and are less able to avoid, or remove themselves from, dangerous situations. The same phenomenon holds for less overtly dangerous treatment by men. If girls grow up in an environment where females are minimized—where women and girls are not listened to, where their ideas are ignored, or they're rewarded or acknowledged for how they look, not what they do—they will be more accepting of this treatment by the males in their lives, whether boyfriends, husbands, bosses, co-workers, or friends.

"I notice how my father and my friends' fathers treat our moms and I think every father should know that their daughters are watching."
—17-year-old survey respondent

"I would tell all fathers to treat their daughters like ladies so they will know how she should be treated by all males."
—15-year-old survey respondent

25. Tell Your Daughter You Love Her

Girls want to hear this from both their parents, but they think it's especially important for fathers to tell them how much they love them. As girls transform from girl to young woman, they become, in ways that first meet the eye, more like their mothers and less like their fathers.

Daughters can misunderstand the separation that occurs when fathers stop feeling comfortable with the more buddy-like relationship they had with their prepubescent daughters. Sometimes girls feel rejected, and sometimes they feel self-conscious and ashamed, wishing things could go back to the way they were when their bodies looked like a boy's body.

Telling her you love her is a way to let her know you care about her and that the changes she is going through don't change how you feel about her.

"Most men are not as good as women in expressing their love, and during adolescence, girls need to hear that both their parents love and support them no matter what."
—18-year-old advisory board member

SPECIAL ADVICE FOR MOTHERS

26. Listen a Lot and Talk a Little

When girls talk with their mothers, they're looking for a way to sort through their experiences with someone they know is similar to them, yet different. That's why a lot of listening goes a long way. Rather than receiving lots of direct advice from their mothers, girls say they like to hear stories of their mothers' experiences that are similar. What went right (and wrong!) in a situation? What would you have done differently? How does your experience seem the same as, or different from, your daughter's?

Girls make a distinction between an adviser and someone who tells them what to do. Advice that is not based on your daughter's experience is seen as "being told what to do," and it is not what girls want. The fine line between "adviser" and "giving advice" is an important one that can be cultivated by listening carefully to your daughter's ideas and experiences and responding to what is going on for her, not what it may seem to be at first glance.

"My mom and I go for long walks every night and I know during those times I can speak freely. My mom responds as a friend and woman, not a questioning parent."
—16-year-old survey respondent

"Mothers should sit down once a week with their daughters and have a conversation about her week. Listen a lot and ask a lot of questions. Avoid giving advice when none is sought."
—17-year-old survey respondent

27. Spend Time Alone with Your Daughter

Girls often talk about feeling invisible. Louder, more boisterous boys may get more attention in the classroom and at home, even if it is attention that tells them to quiet down. Girls, as they hit adolescence, are being noticed for the changes their bodies are going through and often become so self-conscious they wish they were invisible.

But even if they feel invisible in school or social situations, or wish they were invisible when boys make comments about their bodies, they still want to be noticed by people they care about.

If you have other children or an extended family living at home, try to do something once a week alone with your daughter. Girls don't mention big, time-consuming activities when this suggestion comes up. A trip to the mall or a bookstore, a stop at a bakery for

If you doubt that boys receive more attention from teachers, take a look at *School Girls: Young Women, Self-Esteem and the Confidence Gap* (described in the "Gender Equity, Feminism, and Equal Rights" resource listings on page 163) to get a picture of the imbalance that exists and how unaware of it most teachers are.

a treat and conversation, or a walk in the evening all fit the bill. The one activity girls mentioned frequently that might require more planning is an unrushed meal out together. Take the time to talk with your daughter about your lives. Savor what a neat girl she's become, and let her know you think so.

"Surprise your daughter once in a while with a one-on-one meal with no other siblings around."
—17-year-old survey respondent

"If there was one thing I would tell every mother to do for or with her daughter to build her self-confidence, it would be my favorite four-letter word: Talk."
—16-year-old survey respondent

28. Find an Older Woman

Girls want to spend time around adult women other than their mothers. They're interested in finding out what women's lives are like and talking with women, not just their peers, about things like careers and relationships. They also appreciate having a woman they can talk to about things that come up with their own mothers; they recognize the value of getting another adult's perspective rather than their friends'.

Many girls have developed this kind of relationships with women they baby-sit for and with their mothers' friends, but for those who don't have close contact with other older women, seek out special resources. Girls who participate in programs like the Girls Scouts and Girls Incorporated (see "National Organizations" on page 174) often mention that, in addition to benefits of the planned activities, their participation hooked them up with adult women who served as role models and mentors.

The Big Brothers/Big Sisters program is another resource for finding an adult role model for your daughter. (Check the white pages of your phone book to see if there is a program in your area.) Also check with the National Mentoring Partnership (see page 162 for more information) and your daughter's school to see if it offers a mentorship program. Look into *Mother-Daughter Choices: A Hand-*

book for the Coordinator, which provides guidance for a program in which mothers and daughters meet regularly to discuss issues about growing up female in our society. Participants report that their girls often express themselves to, and ask for advice from, the other adult women in the group in ways they don't one-on-one with their mothers. *For All Our Daughters,* an excellent up-to-date exploration of the importance of mentoring for girls, offers lots of insight and advice on getting your daughter involved with women role models. You'll find information about both books in the "Books and Newsletters for Adults" resource listing that starts on page 133.

> Research by the Ms. Foundation found that girls who had a female role model outside the family who talked openly with them and in whom the girls could confide were more confident than girls who did not have a similar role model.

"I want my mom to be sort of cool, but not too cool. I want my mom to be a mom, but I want to be around other cool women too."
—18-year-old advisory board member

29. Do Something for *Yourself*

Girls like to see their moms step outside the role of supermom or superwoman and do something just for themselves. One girl said she felt proud of her mom when she left the dirty dishes in the sink and went out for a horseback ride, one of her favorite activities.

By adolescence, girls have learned the lesson well that women often nurture others, but infrequently nurture themselves. They recognize the mixed blessing of living in a time when women can have it all. They want to know that it's okay to do things only for themselves.

So do your daughter a favor. Stop being the perfect supermom and let her see a woman put herself first once in a while. For practical ideas about how to let go of some things, buy yourself a copy of *Meditations for Women Who Do Too Much* (Anne Wilson Schaef, HarperCollins).

"My mother works and does most of the household chores too. It's hard for her to leave things in a mess, but sometimes I just tell her to and we go out together. I know it's hard for her, but I feel proud of her when she does."

—17-year-old survey respondent

Girl Power!

This chapter wouldn't be necessary if every girl felt the way one survey participant did: "I have never believed in 'Girl Power!' because I have always felt equal to boys."

While we're making progress toward equality, we still need this chapter. Lots of people, including many girls themselves, think girls should be made of sugar and spice and all things nice. But sugar and spice and being nice don't help little girls grow up to be smart, strong, confident women in charge of their lives and destinies: speaking out, playing hard, standing up for yourself, and going for what you want do.

Girl power means taking safe risks and avoiding ones that threaten health and self-esteem. Girls describe safe risk-taking as "putting themselves out there" by assuming leadership roles, performing in public, sharing their writing or art, playing competitive sports, and speaking up against sexism, harassment, and other injustices. These acts build confidence and help girls identify what they care about and how their concerns fit with their daily lives now, and with their dreams and goals for the future.

Girl power also means feeling strong enough to act smart about drugs, cigarettes, violence, alcohol, and sex—even if friends are not. At school and in social situations with peers, girls who get into uncomfortable and risky situations need the tools and confidence to get themselves out.

For girls to be expressive and assertive, they need help. In a society where teenage girls are asked daily to choose between safe and risky behaviors, and where they face mixed messages about women's value and role in society, it's important for girls to have positive feelings about being female. That's the purpose of this chapter: to provide activity ideas that will encourage girls to feel influential, important, appreciated, and optimistic about being a girl and woman in our culture.

> When girls and boys are asked if they would like to become a member of the opposite sex, boys almost universally say no, describing the imagined change as a disadvantage and even reacting to the possibility with disgust. In contrast, girls react favorably to the possibility, citing many advantages.

"Girls should speak out because people will step on you if you don't. If I don't speak up for myself, who will?"
—15-year-old survey respondent

30. Take Her Ideas and Concerns Seriously

Girls want to know they can influence the world around them. In school and often at home, a big part of growing up is spent going along with what is happening, rather than making things happen.

You can play an important role in counteracting this trend by paying careful attention to your daughter's questions and comments and encouraging her to act on them. The pre-teen and teen years are often a period of awakening social awareness for adolescents. Girls who have cooperative and empathetic ways of functioning in the world—whether as a result of nature or nurture or, most probably, both—may experience this earlier or more strongly than boys do.

Your daughter might express concern about animal welfare and decide to become a vegetarian, worry about the homeless children in your town and wish she could do something to help, or read about the testing of cosmetic and pharmaceutical products on animals and decide to boycott products produced by the guilty companies.

Don't pooh-pooh her concerns, or tell her that her ideas are impractical, or that she'll "outgrow it." Celebrate that she is thinking about things, looking for solutions, and willing to act out of commitment. And then go a step further: help her find or organize the resources she needs to act effectively and intelligently. Let her know in every way you can that you respect and appreciate her thoughtfulness, critical thinking, and desire to make a difference.

The ways we have been trained to minimize women's and girls' ideas are subtle. In an interview with gender-equity researcher David Sadker, after the death of his wife and collaborator, Myra, he described how people complained that Myra "talked too much" when the two were interviewed. In fact, they had agreed beforehand that each would speak 50 percent of the time. From these and other experiences in graduate school, in which Myra's equal contribution to research and proposals was virtually ignored, they saw how frequently and insidiously the female "voice" was ignored or silenced.

"Throughout my life my mother has played an important role in supporting my ideas. As young as third grade, when the boys decided to no longer 'allow' the girls to play handball, my mother encouraged me to strike; she left it up to me to take the initiative, but that was the first-ever girl-led strike of the handball court. Through this experience I was able to see a self-directed action create change as well as participate in a positive activity that reinforced my power as a woman."
—18-year-old advisory board member

31. Arrange and Encourage All-Girl Educational and Recreational Experiences

Despite the controversy swirling around the value of single-sex education, girls themselves identify the experience as an important one.

For information about single-sex education, check out the National Coalition of Girls' Schools and a report by the American Association of University Women's report (*Separated by Sex: A Critical Look at Single Sex Education for Girls*). Information about both groups is included in the listing of "National Organizations" on page 174.

If they feel self-conscious around boys, an all-girl environment can provide an opportunity to try their wings with birds of a feather.

Research shows that, in general, girls prefer and perform better in cooperative, rather than competitive, learning environments. When only girls are present, collaboration and cooperation are the mainstays of information gathering, problem-solving, and communication. In a mixed setting, usually based on a more competitive model, these approaches are less available, making the learning process less enjoyable and less effective.

Providing all-girl learning opportunities in the mix of your daughter's activities is a way to help her feel good about her ability to learn. While many girls do enjoy attending an all-girls school, saying it allows them to focus on school and other activities like sports without feeling self-conscious, it may not be practical or desirable for all girls. But there are lots of ways to offer the experience.

Summer camps, particularly ones that center around one topic, like art or science, give girls a chance to pursue an area of interest and meet other girls who are interested in the same topic. Special events also provide all-girl educational opportunities; in my town a Girls' Conference that provided career explorations for 350 middle-school girls was sponsored by a number of local organizations.

For information about all-girl camps check the FeMiNa and Expect the Best from a Girl Web sites in the "Gender Equity, Feminism, and Equal Rights" resource listings on page 163. And if your daughter has an entrepreneurial bent, check out "Organizations and

To get a picture of what girls experience in school settings with boys, read *School Girls: Young Women, Self-Esteem and the Confidence Gap* and *Failing at Fairness*. (Both books are described in the "Books and Newsletters for Adults" resource listings on 133). Both offer compelling, can't-put-it-down accounts of how girls are often ignored by teachers, uninterested in competing for attention against boys' more aggressive styles, and willing to stay—indeed, are often more comfortable—in the background where they can and keep their intelligence out of the spotlight.

Camps" in the "Business and Finance" resource listings that start on page 146. Also visit www.kidscamps.com, where you can search for camps by topic (from art and computers to special needs and science and everything in between), geographic area, and coed or single-sex.

"In middle school, I took a class in women's studies, the only class I ever took that was composed entirely of girls. That was really the first class that I ever felt comfortable voicing my opinion in."
—18-year-old advisory board member

"Girl Scouts definitely gave me the opportunity to cultivate my assertive side. By participating in many all-girl events, I learned to speak out and stand up for myself. I was a member of an acting troupe called Act Out Speak Up that allowed me to show my creative side without being chastised for being disruptive."
—18-year-old survey respondent

"I always feel better about myself when I do things with other girls. That's one reason I chose a women's college, but I've always organized activities with my girlfriends, like making crafts, where it's just us and no guys are invited."
—18-year-old advisory board member

32. Encourage Her to Join the Club

Joining a girls' club provides lots of opportunities to participate in constructive activities with other girls similar to the opportunities offered by the activity suggestion above, but it offers some distinct benefits that warrant giving it special attention.

In a girls' club, girls often develop long-term friendships that can help them remain involved in activities when they hit the common early-adolescence drop-out phase. Dropping out of the club can mean losing friends—a downside that keeps girls going to club meetings for the friendships, with the healthy side effect that they remain active and involved in all kinds of interesting programs.

Girls also meet women who are interested in them and encourage them. The women might be the club leaders, a speaker who comes to a club meeting, or women participants in special programs sponsored by the club. Whatever the setting, girls have opportunities to come into contact with influential women from their community or the national scene during special events. They also participate in diverse experiences that help them understand themselves and how the world works. In a Colorado girls' club event, members got to interview influential women from around the country and write up the interviews to share with others.

Get your daughter involved early in a club and encourage her to stay involved for years. Let her know you think what she's doing is important by volunteering to help, attending special activities, and asking frequently about what she's doing with her club.

The Girl Scouts and Girls Incorporated have branches and clubs throughout the United States. For more information about them, see the listings of "National Organizations" on page 174. There are also many local and state girls' organizations. To find out if there is one in your area, contact the Coalition for America's Children in the listings of "National Organizations." They have state-by-state information about youth organizations.

"Joining an all-girl organization helped me develop a dream and work toward it. I see a lot of strong women who were once just like me. Now they're making a big difference in my community and it encourages me to do the same and not give up on my aspirations."
—20-year-old survey respondent

"I have been in Girl Scouts since I was five and it has truly been a great influence on my life. It's given me the values and ability to know that I can believe in myself under any circumstances."
—18-year-old survey participant

"I've been in Girl Scouts with some of the same girls for years. Knowing someone really well like that and working together to accomplish your goals helps you learn how to set your own goals and work toward them."
—18-year-old editorial board member

33. Give Her Someone to Look Up To

Girls want role models. Knowing there are women and girls who are accomplished, interesting, and committed fuels their optimism, desire, and persistence. Offer your daughter a full plate of female figures to look up to. History, science, politics, art, literature, social activism, and sports are populated with a great cast.

Books, Web sites, magazines, and newspapers are filled with stories about great women, past and present. Gather these resources and fill your daughter's environment with them. Visit the newsstand or library together and pick out magazines that feature stories of accomplished women and girls. Subscribe to one.

Read biographies of women and discuss them. Clip articles from the newspaper and start a scrapbook of stories that feature strong females. When your daughter is looking for a mentor or interested in a subject or career, suggest that she write a letter to one of these local women whose interests are similar to hers. (This is an almost irresistible proposition for most women. I know I thoroughly enjoy it when students interview me about my field.)

For resources to fill your daughter's environment with information about inspiring women and girls, check the listings of "Books about Good Books for Girls" on page 130, "Magazines for Girls" on page 172, and "Gender Equity, Feminism, and Equal Rights" on page 163. Also, check the Web sites and books included in the topic listings "Business and Finance" (page 146), "Math, Science, and Technology" (page 151), and "Sports and Physical Activities" (page 183).

"I realized I could be anything when women started taking giant steps forward. For example, I wanted to be an astronaut, and they sent a black woman into space and I knew I could do it. Then I wanted to be a marine biologist and I began to volunteer at an animal museum. Most of the people working behind the scenes were women, so I knew I could do it. I have always wanted to play pro basketball in the NBA, and they came out with the WNBA, which proved to me that I could do anything."

—17-year-old survey respondent

"Girl Scouts gave me the concept of Girl Power. Everything was girl-oriented and events with important women community leaders were really inspirational and showed you what women could do."
—16-year-old survey respondent

"Recently I participated in a Title IX project where a group of thirty girls interviewed women of achievement. There were many conflicting views and I voiced my opinion. By being aggressive, I got to interview Jane Fonda!"
—18-year-old survey respondent

34. Mothers, Speak Up!

One of the most influential factors girls talk about that gave them the courage to speak up and take control of situations is having assertive women as their role models. Mothers, teachers, friends, and public figures are all in girls' lines of sight.

As a mom, you can model assertiveness in many contexts: at home, in social situations, in stories you tell about work or volunteer activities, and in your activities with your daughter. For most of us, this isn't always easy. Women and girls learn well to defer, go along, and do what's best for the group or others. There's nothing inherently wrong with doing what's best for the group or others, but when it is at the expense of the individual, there are costs. The costs may be emotional and psychological, or they may be physical, if a girl finds herself unable to speak up and resist peer pressure.

Being assertive doesn't mean things always go your way—nor should it. It means taking the risk and making the effort to let others know what you think. The outcome might be going to a movie that's not your first pick because everyone else wants to go to another one, but you do it openly and freely after expressing what you really want. The outcome might be that you choose not to participate in an event because people are not being treated fairly, or you change the way things are done by expressing your misgivings. Your daughter is watching you in these situations, and what she sees has an effect on her.

But don't just stop at observation. Let her know that sometimes it's hard for you to speak up. Sometimes you're not even sure exactly what you think or feel, but you need to sort it out so you don't regret something done (or undone) down the road. Encourage her to bring similar dilemmas to you.

> If you have trouble speaking up, try reading *Self-Assertion for Women* (Pamela Butler, Harper) and *Good Girls Go to Heaven, Bad Girls Go Everywhere: How to Break the Rules and Get What You Want from Your Job, Your Family and Your Relationship* (Jana Ehrhardt, St. Martin's Press). They'll help you understand what assertiveness is, how it's different from aggression, and offer specific behaviors and phrases you can use to train yourself to be assertive.

"A daughter's biggest possible role model is her mother. A positive, confident mother makes a positive, confident daughter."
—18-year-old survey respondent

35. Ask for Her Opinion

The underlying theme of this book is the idea that girls are thoughtful and interesting. Adults can learn a lot by listening carefully to them, and they can foster girls' sense of positive power by acknowledging their ideas. Asking girls for their opinion is one of the easiest ways to get these two benefits.

When your daughter comes to you to report something that happened, perhaps at school or with a friend, ask her what she thinks of the incident or how she feels about it before you jump in with a reaction. Continue questioning her in a friendly, curious way and comment that her perspective is thoughtful or interesting.

When something out of the ordinary happens to you, a friend, or a sibling, describe the situation to her and ask her what she thinks about it. You'll get to know and understand her better, while opening the door to a self-image for her that says, "What I think matters."

Extend this kind of interest in her opinions to other topics. Encourage her to think about the community and political arena by reading her a short article from the paper and getting her opinion about the events. Use a friendly, curious approach that shows you're interested in her ideas, not looking for a debate.

Asking her opinion also extends to including her in discussions about events that affect her life on a more personal level. Where should the family go for the summer vacation? Who would she like to include in holiday gatherings? Are there family friends she would like to get together with more often? If the family is making a major purchase, like a car, what does she think might meet everyone's needs? Let her know she has influence over her world, and that her opinion counts.

This kind of solicitation and consideration of her ideas will go a long way toward giving her the confidence and self-esteem she needs to speak up in class, clubs, social situations, and extracurricular activities.

"Respect your daughter's opinions and encourage her to form her own."
—18-year-old advisory board member

"Treat your daughter like an intelligent, inquiring human being."
—17-year-old survey respondent

36. Get Her in the Game

Participating in sports was the most common activity girls cited in the survey that gave them "Girl Power!" Certainly, not every girl is interested in sports, but for those who are—and more and more are—participation has an enormous positive effect.

Whether they go for team or individual sports, girls are articulate about what their participation does for them: "It gives me confidence I can achieve"; "My favorite sport is tennis and when I play with my guy friends they get really competitive because they don't want to be beaten by a girl. It's awesome when I do"; "Basketball taught me it's okay for girls to be aggressive, even off the court."

For girls involved in team sports, there can be other benefits too, from learning about teamwork and leadership to being motivated to work hard to accomplish goals.

"Softball has changed my life. I love the sport and the whole team acts like sisters. What's so good about it that it's an all-girls thing. We have girl power and the club has inspired me to be a better person."
—16-year-old survey respondent

"Even though I had to deal with a lot of small-town politics and a horrible coach, I worked my way up to a number-seven spot on the tennis team. When one of my teammates was injured, I played the number-four singles spot. To be able to be a contributing member of the team was a big moment in my life when I felt strong and thankful for how hard I had worked for my goal."
—18-year-old survey respondent

And for girls who may not feel they're up to the challenge, or it's just not their thing, it's worth a try. They might be surprised at the satisfaction they feel and the fun they have, even if they're not a natural or a superstar.

"When I joined the badminton team, I wasn't as physically fit as the other girls, so I was very discouraged in the beginning. But my coach was great and after I got to know everyone, I really enjoyed myself and my self-esteem was boosted up an entire level."
—16-year-old survey respondent

Parents can have a strong influence on girls' desire to participate in sports. Research indicates that adult comments influence girls' desire to start or continue in sports, and this is particularly true for

Take a visit to the Nike Web site (in the "Sports and Physical Activities" resource listings on page 183), where girls can find out what women athletes are thinking and doing and read first-hand accounts of other teenage girls' sports participation. Lots of other Web sites of interest are included in this listing, along with good books on the topic. Also, check out girls' programs offered by the Women's Sports Foundation and the National Association for Women and Girls in Sport, both of which are also described in the "Sports and Physical Activities" resource listings.

In a review of sports research, the Women's Sports Foundation found that half of all girls who participate in sports have higher than average levels of self-esteem and less depression than their nonplaying counterparts. They are also less likely to become involved with drugs or become pregnant, and are more likely to graduate from high school.

pre-teen girls, who are most influenced by their parents. Talk about the benefits and fun that can be derived from sports, participate yourself, and offer lots of opportunities for your daughter to try out different activities so she has a good chance of finding one she really enjoys and will want to stick with.

37. Talk About and Analyze How Girls and Women Are Portrayed

Girls want their parents—and other significant adults in their lives—to take an interest in how girls and women are portrayed in the media and in other materials. Ask to see your daughter's history and social studies textbooks. Find out whose works are studied in literature, music, and art classes. In science classes, are women's contributions discussed? You may be surprised, in an era when women do enjoy many fruits of the feminist movement, at the paucity of women portrayed.

In an analysis of high-school history textbooks, researchers Myra and David Sadker found that less than 3 percent of one book referred to women; another less than 2 percent. And these texts were described as "inclusive" by the publishers. (For more information about the Sadkers' work, see *Failing at Fairness*, described in "Gender Equity, Feminism, and Equal Rights" on page 163. In this resource listing, also check out the Women's History Project, where you can order great books, posters, T-shirts, and other products about women and girls who have made a difference.

Right alongside the limited academic portrayal of women, the popular media presents an equally distorted view. While more television shows and movies feature female protagonists than was the case in the past, there are few realistic portrayals. No matter what the women and girls are doing, being beautiful and thin are still most often prerequisites for the role. The message comes across that girls and women first must "be" (thin and beautiful), while men can get credit right out of the gate for what they "do." Also look at what all the women and girls are doing and how they are talking. Are they speaking up and out? Are they deferential to men? And television and magazine ads barely deserve mention: attractive women are used to sell everything from beer to cigarettes and cars. Keep a pad by the TV and make a check every time an ad featuring a bimbo appears. How many times an hour do they appear? Keep a similar bimbo log for magazines. You'll be surprised by the count, even in magazines that include articles about accomplished women.

You have lots of resources to help counteract the bombardment of unrealistic images and roles your daughter faces. Start with magazines like *Teen Voices* or *New Moon*. (See page 172 for a list of girls' magazines that show them as strong, diverse, and active.) Pick up some books for her like *A Girls' Guide to Life* and *Girl Talk: Staying Strong, Feeling Good, Sticking Together*. You'll find these and others described in the list of "Books for Girls" on page 125. Also look through the listing on "Body Image and Media Representation of Women" (page 140) where you'll find out about organizations like Media Watch and About-Face that track and critique the media's representation of women. And last but not least, fire up a computer and visit Girls Incorporated's Web site (www.girlsinc.org) where you'll find Girls Re-Cast TV Action Kit, an on-line activity to help you evaluate what you see on television.

38. March Together

Pre-adolescence and adolescence are often a time of growing awareness of social injustice and empathy for the less privileged. You can forge a bond with your daughter and raise awareness and sometimes money for worthy causes by beating the pavement together. (And you get some exercise in the bargain.)

Around the country, there are marches specifically for women's causes, like Race for the Cure to fight breast cancer, and Take Back the Night, which works to educate about and prevent rape. These can have special meaning for mother-daughter walkers, but other walks and marches, including fund-raising walkathons like those sponsored to raise funds to fight cystic fibrosis, can bring daughters and their mothers and fathers closer together, and support girls' interests in making a difference in the world.

Try inviting some of the men and boys in your life too, particularly to events like Take Back the Night, whose long-term success depends on educating and influencing men and boys.

"One of our friends had breast cancer and that got my mother and me started in participating in the Race for the Cure. I liked it that I was helping other women and it was fun to be in this big crowd of people who were all there for the same reason."
—16-year-old survey respondent

39. Encourage Her to Work for Causes She Believes In

Activities girls cited in this area include everything from working to improve migrant labor working conditions, AIDS awareness education, and serving Thanksgiving dinner to the homeless to organizing Earth Week events. Girls want to feel influential. They want to know that what they do makes a difference and that they're helping make the world the kind of place they want to live in. Also important in these activities is the knowledge girls acquire about people and issues they didn't know about before.

When girls work for a cause they believe in, they're letting other people know where they stand and that they are willing to be noticed for it, maybe even disapproved of by some who disagree with them. It may be speaking out for lesbian rights, affiliating with a political party or an issue that is not supported by a majority in her community, or pushing to work on a cause that many might prefer to ignore, like homelessness. Whatever the cause or issue, speaking out holds some risk. Recognize this fact and support and encourage your daughter.

"Activism in high school helped me find my voice and learn to use it. I went from being shy and terrified of public speaking to teaching workshops and answering a crisis line."
—18-year-old advisory board member

"I participated in World AIDS Day, and I felt it was a way to speak out about a crisis affecting my peers and race. I want to know everything there is to know about this deadly disease."
—16-year-old survey respondent

There are lots of resources to encourage and support your daughter's efforts. Almost all the magazines in the list of "Magazines for Girls" on page 172 include frequent articles about causes girls can become involved in and descriptions of real projects. *The Kid's Guide to Social Action* (described in the "Activism" resource list on page 119) is a complete handbook for identifying a good cause to work on, developing an action plan, and tapping into helpful resources. The "Activism" resource listings also describe a great little newsletter called *Things I Must Do Today* that is filled with ideas for affecting the world, along with information about lots of organizations and Web sites about social issues. Many high schools around the country now require students to do a certain number of hours of community service in order to graduate. If this is the case for your daughter, help her identify a good project that will be rewarding and educational.

40. Encourage Her to Work for Women's Rights

This activity idea is distinct from the previous one because it has such significance for girls. Girls are naturally interested in women and girls, and their involvement in women's rights can be an initiation into how their world is different from the world as men and boys experience it.

When girls get involved in women's rights, it is often an introduction to facts about women's lives—like the discrepancy in pay scales for men and women—that cry out for action. Or it may be that the facts come first. Finding out that over 300,000 women are raped each year can be a call to action. You can spark her interest in these issues by pointing out related articles in the newspaper and discussing them.

For girls, involvement can mean meeting accomplished, compelling women who serve as role models or mentors, forging a special connection with other women and girls, making friends with other girls who share their concerns, and learning that their actions and ideas can make a difference.

In exciting trends, girls are being called on to make a contribution to girls' rights. The Fourth World Conference on Women in Beijing in 1995 included a Platform for Action for girls in which girls themselves participated. Girls Speak Out (see the "National Organizations" list on page 174) sponsors girls' conferences in which their ideas are solicited for an agenda to improve the lives of girls. The National Organization for Women (NOW) (on page 163 in the "Gender Equity, Feminism, and Equal Rights" resource listings) encourages girls to start local chapters and offers guidance. While you're looking up NOW, also check out the Feminist Majority Foundation and feminist.com (included in the same resource listing), where you'll find information about a wide range of women's causes to get involved in.

"My most educational experience has been petitioning for the United Nations Convention for the Elimination of All Forms of Discrimination Against Women (CEDAW). The petitioning has definitely fostered my leadership and social skills and taught me the need for women's equality worldwide."
—20-year-old survey respondent

"Working in a shelter for battered women has made me more of an activist and influenced my career goals. I want to do something that will improve conditions for girls and women."
—18-year-old advisory board member

41. Encourage Cooperation with Boys

Cooperation, appreciation, and respect between boys and girls can have a profound effect on how girls experience themselves in the world. (And how boys experience themselves—which, of course, affects how girls experience themselves.) Girls don't want the control of their lives to come at the expense of boys' confidence or control. They want their desire to pursue the physical and intellectual activities that interest and challenge them to be accepted.

Respectful, cooperative relations can start at home if you have sons and daughters. Take heed of Activity No. 19's suggestion to treat girls and boys equally. Girls who grew up with brothers say the contact gave them an ability to stand up for themselves around their guy friends and kid without letting it get out of control. For families with no boys, seek out special activities (like those described in the sidebar near the bottom of the page) where girls and boys work together to accomplish goals. In these goal-directed settings, girls will have an opportunities to express and defend their opinions and ideas.

If you have sons or are involved with boys and young men and want some guidance in helping them develop, take a look at *Real Boys: Rescuing Our Sons from the Myths of Boyhood* (William Pollack, Random House) and *A Fine Young Man: What Parents, Mentors and Educators Can Do to Shape Adolescent Boys into Exceptional Men* (Michael Gurian, TarcherPutman).

As a role model for your daughter, speak to and treat boys respectfully and comment to your daughter about men and boys who treat women and girls well. It will foster her awareness and encourage her to start the ball rolling in that direction. If you're "marching" together, invite boys and men to join you. Ask them if you can join a cause or group they are involved in to lend support to issues they care about.

Campfire Boys and Girls, which started out as an all-girl organization but later opened its doors to boys, encourages all young people to work together. For more information about the organization's youth camps, leadership development, and other activities, see page 175 in the "National Organizations" resource listings.

"I learned to be competitive with guys in soccer, but it's important to work harmoniously with them too. When I was petitioning for the United Nations Convention for the Elimination of All Forms of Dis-

crimination Against Women, it became obvious that men need to stand behind the efforts too."

—20-year-old survey respondent

"I grew up in a family with a lot of brothers. It has definitely helped me learn to stand up for myself and get along with guys to get things done."

—18-year-old editorial board member

42. Find Some Younger Girls

Just as girls want interaction with "an older" woman (Activity No. 28), they also enjoy having a positive influence on younger girls.

For girls in their early teens, baby-sitting, serving as a camp or park counselor or volunteer, and spending time with siblings and friends' siblings all offer ways to fulfill this desire. As girls get older, many of the organizations they belong to provide avenues for their interest in helping younger girls. The Girl Scouts, for example, actively encourages older members to organize scouting events for younger girls.

Helping younger girls is also a great outlet for activists who want to work for causes they believe in. For example, one of my advisory board members organized educational activities for younger girls on eating disorders, AIDS prevention, and a variety of other sensitive issues. These activities provided the basis for her senior project, a college-type term paper required for graduation.

Encourage and help with resources for any and all of these kinds of interests. Serving as a role model and mentor to younger girls will build both your daughter's and the younger girls' self-esteem and confidence. If you have an interest in working with girls' organizations, serving as a sports coach, or in some other way organizing or supervising girls' activities, do it! You'll be a great role model for your daughter and she may decide she wants to come along to help.

"When a younger girl I know asked me to come speak in her class about some things I had done, I thought, That's me she looks up to. I'm her role model. It felt really good, and then when I saw how shy she was when she introduced me to her class, I realized that she was taking a

risk inviting me and it was encouraging her to take risks and be pro-
active.
—18-year-old editorial board member

"Girls and Women in Sports Day is a great activity. I volunteered at
the college to help with this program and the little girls all seemed so
excited. They were able to challenge themselves with new and exciting
games that have previously been called 'boys' sports."
—16-year-old survey respondent

"I volunteered to be an assistant camp counselor with girls who came
from foster homes, who had been raped or other things. I realized that
despite the fact that I only had a week, I could really affect these girls
for that entire week. I forgot all about my own needs and focused on
them. Helping those girls helped me by showing me that I could make
a difference."
—18-year-old survey respondent

43. Let Her Know It's Not Just a Guy Thing

Is your daughter interested in weight-lifting, running for class president, or starting a computer club? Are these things most often done
by boys in her social group or school? Encourage her to break the
mold. Confident girls enjoy—even savor—the challenge of showing
boys they can do anything.

In sports, girls chafe at boys telling them they "wouldn't make
the team," "shouldn't take weight-lifting," or "didn't know how to
play." The boys' comments stimulated them to try harder and they
proudly report that they did "make the team," "get the grade in
weight lifting," or become "a great dribbler in basketball."

Knowing they have something to prove gets the "play hard"
juices flowing. And not just in sports. Fund-raising, planning special
events, and running for school office are all things girls mention
when talking about the satisfaction they derive from making it in a
"guys' world."

In addition to the confidence girls get from competing with boys,
they can learn another important message. One respondent to the
survey described her reluctance to continue in a school office election

when she learned a guy she liked was running for the same office. She was afraid that if she won, it would ruin her chances with him. She went ahead anyway and found out, "Much to my surprise, I gained more respect from my defeated opponent. And even though I never got the guy, I was right to decide not to withdraw and wrong to assume how he would react."

Recognize that when girls take on the challenge of proving themselves in this way, they may not always come out on top. Let them know that their attitude, effort, and commitment count for more than the end result.

"I'm in charge, with some other girls, of Raza Day. This is the first year it is run by all girls and we heard that it wasn't going to come out good because girls are running it. We already have the day planned out and it is going to be very exciting thanks to the GIRLS!"
—16-year-old survey respondent

"Girls need to stand up for what they believe. A lot of times they sit back and let the guys take over. Girls should get involved and not let guys get in the way. Every now and then I feel like I can't do it, it's a guy thing, but in my mind I tell myself I can. And about seven times out of ten, I can!"
—15-year-old survey respondent

44. Let Her Lead

Leadership takes many forms. Some people lead by marching in front of the ranks, others by expressing their opinions and ideas forthrightly, and still others by quiet example. But girls who feel influential in a group and know they have made a positive difference like the feeling.

Leading is about feeling influential, feeling that you can effect events and make a difference in how people think about things or how events unfold. For girls who do not naturally gravitate toward leadership roles in school or other activities, you can help them feel influential at home by giving them leadership roles. Start small: Find out what her dream day would be and tell her it's hers if she does the planning.

48

Graduate to having your daughter organize more complicated activities or a weekend trip with friends.

Encourage her to join groups like the Girl Scouts, Girls Incorporated, and Campfire Boys and Girls, which work specifically to foster leadership skills. (See the listing of "National Organizations" on page 174 for more information about these groups.)

Let your daughter know girls can make a difference. Check out *Girls and Young Women Leading the Way: 20 True Stories About Leadership* (in the "Activism" resource listings on page 119), which includes tips and resources to help girls lead the way in their own communities. The "Gender Equity, Feminism, and Equal Rights" resource listings on page 163 also offers lots of ways to inspire and encourage leadership skills. *Girls Who Rocked the World: Heroines from Sacajawea to Sheryl Swoopes* lets girls know they can make a difference at any age. *Profiles of Women Past and Present* and other books in the listing offer role models. Read and discuss some of these books with your daughter. For older girls who have feminist or political leadership aspirations, check out the Feminist Majority Leadership Internship and the National Organization for Women, which are described in the same resource listings.

"Running for Student Advisory Council was a big risk that helped build up my confidence. Passing out cards and what-not helped me get to know more people and the campaign was fun, except for the anxiety about the results. The risk was well worth it, though, because of all the fun I've had this year on Student Advisory Council."
—16-year-old survey respondent

"I have been involved in every program Girls Incorporated has and it has had a big impact on my life. It's helped me keep a positive lifestyle and motivated me to take my education seriously. By holding leadership roles, I felt confident and like a role model."
—19-year-old survey respondent

"I was required to complete 100 hours of community service (a requirement for graduation) and for part of it, I was a counselor at a camp for

'underprivileged' kids. This opportunity gave me the chance to be someone's leader and to help those in need."
—17-year-old survey respondent

45. Take Her to the Voting Booth

In a period with one of the lowest voter-turnout rates in thirty years, girls need to know their vote counts. Women's right to vote was hard-won itself and has most certainly been a factor in many of the subsequent rights we take for granted, from reproductive rights to requirements in the workplace that new mothers be granted a leave without risk of losing their jobs.

> Census Bureau data show that the 1996 presidential election had the lowest voter-turnout rate since 1964, when the bureau first began collecting voter-turnout data.

Look over the voter's pamphlet together. Talk about her ideas on each issue. Read the "for" and "against" arguments and consider them with her. Do they make sense? How are they flawed? Do they conflict with your basic values? Talk about how the issues might affect her life and yours.

On election day, take her to your polling place. Let her see how the process works and what the booth and ballot look like. Follow the results in the news. If it's a big enough election that there is television coverage, make some popcorn and watch the results together. Invite some other people over who are also interested. Discuss the results and what they mean.

"My mother started taking me to the polling place when I was eight. I was really interested in everything that went on there and as soon as I was old enough, I registered to vote as soon as I could."
—18-year-old editorial board member

46. Open Doors to the Community

For girls to get involved in meaningful activities and meet interesting people who can have a positive influence on their lives, they need to be exposed to lots of possible choices. Go to public events with her, take her to your company picnics and neighborhood potlucks, participate in religious, cultural, or ethnic celebrations and events. These experiences open doors to possibilities she may not have imagined.

Art, music, and dance festivals, pet parades, 4-H events, rodeos, public talks by noteworthy men and women, and special events at the public library are just a few of the kinds of events girls mentioned in their surveys had helped them find an activity they love.

Notice how your daughter reacts to each experience. Does she ask a lot of questions about it? Does she want to go again? These are good clues that something about the experience resonated with her dreams and talents. Support her interest by brainstorming with her about how she can become involved. What did she like most? What would she like to do to help? Does she have her own idea she wants to propose or does she want to help with an ongoing activity? Once she knows what kinds of activities she'd like to be involved in, she may need help figuring out how to do it. Many things adults take for granted may be a mystery to her. One girl talked about how it was an "aha" experience for her when she realized that someone's office number usually indicated which floor he or she was on, making it easier for her to get to appointments on time. Another tricky issue can be finding an organization's phone number, especially if it's a public or government agency. How do those pages in the front of the phone book work anyway? Many of the mundane things we, as adults, take for granted, can be stumbling blocks for them in working toward larger goals. Help her to stay on track toward her larger goals by guiding her through some of the more mundane tasks we take for granted. For more complicated activities, try some trial runs like those described in Activity No. 52.

An important side benefit that a number of girls mentioned from getting out and finding out about what's available in the community was that the activity became the start of some family traditions. The annual music festival, rodeo, or dog parade became a fun event to look forward to going to with the family.

51

"One of the things that helped me learn more about myself and what I want out of life was joining the National Puerto Rican Day Parade, Inc., to prepare for the parade held every year in New York City. I also participated in the Miss Teenage Puerto Rican Day Parade Pageant, which doesn't revolve around beauty. It focuses on enhancing Puerto Ricans' knowledge of their culture. When I was Miss Teenage Puerto Rico, I devoted my time to educating others about what I learned, and showing them that beauty and body are not as important as intelligence."
—17-year-old survey respondent

47. Notice What She Loves

Does your daughter doodle? Does she have her nose in a book every chance she gets? Catch the beat of the music before you can blink an eye? Love to sit around the table with you and your friends after dinner to talk politics? Hatch moneymaking ideas at the drop of a hat? Hop on her bike for a two-miler when she has free time?

Observing and valuing these natural inclinations offer windows into a world that makes her feel good and competent. Acknowledge, respect, and support those inclinations.

Girls say they think every girl needs something special she's good at. They enjoy and appreciate encouragement from their parents: a drawing pad and pen set for the doodler, a new book for the avid reader, a bike accessories catalog for the cyclist, an offer to help research leadership camps with a budding politician. This show of interest and encouragement strengthens her desire to continue the activity and become more accomplished in it.

"I enjoyed writing poetry and this activity helped me with my confidence and self-esteem because I got noticed by friends, family, and teachers. This helped me because people saw a part of me they hadn't known before."
—20-year-old survey respondent

There are organizations and opportunities galore to encourage your daughter's interests. If she is a budding writer or artist, review the "Self-Expression" resource listings on page 179. For the entrepreneurially inclined, check out the "Business and Finance" list on page 146. For young athletes, try "Sports and Physical Activities" on page 183, and for the young scientist or techno-wiz, take a look at the "Math, Science, and Technology" listings on page 151. Also, review "Magazines for Girls" on page 172. (Most of these magazines include girls' writing and artwork.) To find specialized camps, visit www.kidscamps.com, the Expect the Best from a Girl Web site (www.academic.org), and www.femina.com. Also check your public library FOR FREE *(and almost free) Adventures for Teenagers* (Gail Grand, John Wiley & Sons). Since the book was published in 1995, you'll need to check whether some of the programs are still in existence, but it's worth exploring the many interesting options, from summer-research internships for girls interested in science and engineering to high-school journalism workshops and international communications simulations conducted via the Internet.

48. If She Loves It, Help Her Share It

Encouragement to share her talents, expertise, and enthusiasm with others goes hand-in-hand with helping your daughter become engaged in and committed to something she loves. Being the focus of others' attention is risky business. (For adults as well as young women: adults rank public speaking above death as one of their greatest fears.)

But taking the risk is important for girls. Members of my advisory board describe it as "putting yourself out there," where other people will notice you, and where there is the possibility of both positive recognition, and one of life's most embarrassing moments. The tension inherent in the situation is an incentive to practice hard and perform well. The skill-building and confidence that come from preparation for the event contribute to girls' sense of power as much as the outcome of the event. And not doing so great doesn't mean an end to the activity. One girl who has a knack for organizing ideas and information talked about how her voice quivered when she first began to give talks, but she stuck to it and now, at age eighteen, is practically on the lecture circuit, speaking to local service and business groups about her work with the Red Cross, the Girl Scouts, and her participation in other special events, like carrying the Olympic torch.

> There are myriad ways to help your daughter put herself "out there," whether she is a budding writer, visual or performing artist, politician, social activist, teacher, or athlete. All the resource listings in the sidebar on page 53 include information about ways your daughter can participate in contests or submit her work for publication in magazines or on Web sites. Also, check out the "National Organizations" list on page 174. Programs like the Afro-Academic, Cultural, Technological and Scientific Olympics and leadership and activity opportunities with the Girl Scouts and Girls Incorporated offer many opportunities for girls to be recognized for their efforts and accomplishments. Also look at the Feminist Majority Leadership Internship and the National Organization for Women in the "Gender Equity, Feminism, and Equal Rights" resource listings (page 163) for activity ideas.

"My mother told me one day, 'You can do that!' when I told her about an art contest in middle school. I entered and won first place. I know I wouldn't have done it if she hadn't encouraged me."
—18-year-old editorial board member

"By nature, I am a shy person. It took all my courage to sign up for public speaking class. The class turned out to be quite fun. I learned to be assertive, how to voice my opinions, and how to go after my dreams. The skills I learned have carried over into my life because it made me realize I can do anything I set my mind to."
—16-year-old survey respondent.

49. Buy Your Daughter a Journal

Writing about experiences, ideas, and feelings can be a great source of insight and self-acceptance for girls. A journal is a private place where girls can explore and make sense of the often confusing things that happen at school, with peers, with their parents, and to their bodies and emotions.

Girls talk about treating their journals like a friend. In it they can work out conflicts with friends by writing about the situation, when they're down they go to their journal to express their fears, and they can write about their dreams and hopes. One girl uses her journal to record interesting quotes and returns to them for inspiration when the need strikes.

And for some girls, a journal is the beginning of a lifelong love of writing that remains an avenue for personal expression or can even become a career.

"I use my journal a lot when I'm confused or upset about something. Not really other times, but it helps me sort things out."
—18-year-old editorial board member

To get her started, buy her a copy of *Totally Private & Personal: Journaling Ideas for Girls and Young Women* (see page 179 in the "Self Expression" resource listing). Written by a teenager, girls will be able to relate to the author's suggestions and ideas for making the experience meaningful. Lots of fun journals are available, but for some designed with the adolescent girl in mind, take a look at the New Moon catalog (page 173 in the "Magazines for Girls" listing) or check out their Web site at www.newmoon.org.

50. Document Her Accomplishments

Have you ever come across some old photos, college papers, sketch pads, or other items that document your life? Most people do at some point and are usually enthralled. Even if mortification plays a big part in your response, the "stuff" is proof that you really did those things.

Girls want that proof too. In a world where it's easy for girls to get lost in the crowd, photos and "stuff" can be tangible proof that they are interesting people doing interesting things. Keep a camera or camcorder loaded and capture events that have special meaning or in which your daughter has excelled. For a change, don't recycle!

Keep a permanent collection instead. Pick out things you want to keep, and ask her what she would like to have included. Once a year haul it all out and have a nostalgia party. Talk about the events and objects and their significance in your daughter's life. Keep reminding her that she's neat, capable, and accomplished.

"My parents took lots of pictures of me at different events and have kept a box of my school and hobby projects. It means a lot to me that they did. I feel really good when we look through it."
—19-year-old survey respondent

51. Make Her Uncomfortable

Most adults recognize that growth often comes from pushing old limits and testing comfortable boundaries. Is your daughter resting easy in areas where she would benefit from some challenge? Maybe it's time for a change.

Help your daughter identify areas where she's cruising or avoiding something she's afraid of. Is she technophobic? So painfully shy she avoids activities she enjoys because she's uncomfortable in a group? Coasting in math class when she should be taking something harder? A self-described klutz who would never dare to join a sports team? Start with a comment about something you've avoided because you were afraid to try and ask her if there's something like that in her life. (Don't figure it all out for her and sign her up for something because it will be good for her. Even if she goes in body, she won't be there in spirit.) If she draws a blank, ask her if you can suggest something you think you've noticed.

Work together to find ways to help her push past her comfort zone. Maybe the two of you can take a class together, with the understanding that there'll be a special dinner out at the end to talk over every gruesome detail—or how much fun it turned out to be. Dare each other to do one of the things that haunts you and, again, plan a special reward for afterward. Or if one of you fails, spend a day waiting on the other hand and foot. Take the dread out and put the activity in a context of fun and experimentation. And show that you're willing to make yourself uncomfortable too!

"Taking harder classes makes me feel good about myself because it doesn't matter what I look like. I have that 'smart' feeling inside."
—18-year-old survey respondent

"If you take chances, you will always grow as a person, no matter what the outcomes."
—16-year-old survey respondent

52. Test the Waters with Trial Runs

When your daughter is going out into the world or trying a new activity, remember that she may never have seen or done any of the things she's about to become involved in. A trial run can be the perfect way to increase her confidence before the event, and it can give her the knowledge she needs to handle the real thing.

Trial runs might include role-playing a job interview, casing out the business or organization before an appointment so she has a picture of what it looks like, doing a walk-through of checking in at the airport, filling out a sample bank-account application to find out what sort of information she needs to gather, or visiting a camp before sending her off.

When it's not possible to do a real trial run, do an imaginary one instead. Things she's unsure of, or confused or misinformed about, will come up. When you do your trial run, talk yourselves through the whole experience together until your daughter has a clear picture of what is involved.

"Before my first Wider Opportunities trip in the Girl Scouts, my mother and grandmother took me to the airport and we went through everything I needed to know. I felt pretty comfortable on the first trip and now I've flown so much, I'm more comfortable than lots of adults."
—18-year-old editorial board member

53. Help Her Organize Experiences in Self-Reliance

One girl, who had grown up hiking with her father, used that shared experience to become even more confidant and self-reliant. In a carefully orchestrated and controlled experience, she and a teenage girlfriend hiked a wilderness area for a week. Before the hike, she carefully planned the route with her father, setting checkpoints along the way. Every several days the girls would meet a parent at a specified point along the way, check in, and pick up additional supplies. At the end of the hike, the girls' parents were there to pick them up.

This hike embodies the characteristics of the type of self-reliance experience girls can benefit from. Similar to a Girl Scout cruise my editorial board took, for which they planned and raised money for several years, it required planning before the event, cooperation and communication with others, and identifying and gathering necessary resources.

Talk with your daughter to identify things she's interested in that lend themselves to a planned experience in self-reliance. A few of the things girls mention in this vein include cooking a holiday meal, bike touring, hiking, camping, planning a party or family event, and traveling to a different city for an educational or recreational activity. Plan the event with her, starting with a discussion of who will be involved. Then move on to all the steps and resources that will be needed, including ways to handle things that don't go according to plan. Monitor your own input and reactions to her ideas; listen carefully and ask questions about issues you are concerned about. Don't jump in with answers and solutions. To gain confidence and belief in herself that she can pull off something difficult and important, she needs to be calling the shots.

And when she's finished with the activity, don't forget to celebrate her success and acknowledge her intelligence and ability to make positive things happen for herself.

"My parents nurtured me to do the brave thing. They didn't baby me or do things for me but always helped me build up my endurance so I could fend for myself."
　　—18-year-old editorial board member

"Solving your daughter's problems won't help her in the end. There's a fine line between helping and doing. Let her work it out."
　　—18-year-old survey respondent

54. Don't Just Say No to Drugs

Resisting peer pressure and media influence can take lots of girl power, and when it comes to drugs, girls want knowledge, not scare tactics, from their parents. One girl said her parents' credibility went way up when they researched drug topics with her; when they found out together what effects specific drugs have and what the dangers can be, it was no longer an issue of her parents warning her. The facts and the information persuaded her.

> In a study by the Center for Substance Abuse Prevention, teens said they didn't think parents were credible when they talked about drugs. Teens particularly disliked scare tactics as a way to discourage them from using drugs.

Girls also say that many—though certainly not all—of the kids in school who do use drugs and alcohol have very strict parents. These kids seem to fall prey to the taboo effect: The more parents say don't, the more kids want to. Many of the girls on my advisory board say they are allowed to sip wine with their parents on special occasions. As a result, it doesn't seem like something off limits and they are not attracted to doing it just because they aren't supposed to. The psychology of taboo means that kids often try something simply because they are not supposed to. Don't add to the mystique by "just saying no." Research the effects of drugs and alcohol with your daughter and talk with her about what you find.

Include research about smoking in your efforts. The trend of reduced teen smoking seen in the eighties is reversing itself, with serious lifelong health consequences for girls: the National Center on Addiction and Substance Abuse found that more women die from lung cancer than breast cancer. In the nineties smoking has been glamorized in not so subtle ways (the Joe Camel campaign), and in more subtle ways: *Health* magazine reported that in the 1970s and '80s, someone smoked or referred to smoking in a film an average of eight times. In the '90s: twenty-five times.

For information about a drug prevention program targeted to teenage girls, contact Girls Incorporated (see page 176) and check out the Department of Health and Human Services' Girl Power campaign (see page 192).

For information about the effects of drugs, see *Drug and Alcohol Abuse: The Authoritative Guide for Parents, Teachers and Counselors; Taking Charge of My Mind and Body: A Girls' Guide to Outsmarting Alcohol, Drugs, Smoking and Eating Problems;* and related books. The U.S. Department of Health and Human Services' National Clearinghouse for Alcohol and Drugs also has information on its Web site (www.health.org) about the effects of drugs, and the National Center for Tobacco-Free Kids sponsors a Kick Butt campaign. (Information about these books and programs is included in the "Staying Safe and in Control" resource listings on page 188.)

55. Show Her the Seamy Side of Life

One of the challenges many adults face in trying to influence teen behavior is the "immortality" phenomenon: Kids believe they are immune to disease, death, and bodily harm, especially if it's something that might not occur until twenty years down the road.

The phenomenon is a mixed blessing of youth. Without it, teens might be less inclined to stretch and take risks that encourage growth. With it, they are at risk for so many potentially life-threatening possibilities it boggles the mind.

One thing girls say does affect their thinking and behavior is "up close and personal" exposure to the things that put them at risk. One girl described how her grandfather suffered from lung cancer and general ill health after a lifetime of smoking and alcohol abuse. She watched as he sickened and lingered, smelled and sounded bad, and finally succumbed. When other teens are drinking or using drugs, she doesn't, even in the face of being teased at times. Interestingly, a quick way she's found to stop the ribbing is to explain why she abstains.

Driving is another activity that can be influenced by what girls call "realistic images." As with drugs, scare tactics and vague descriptions of the consequences of being reckless behind the wheel don't have much credibility. Seeing firsthand what can happen does. Some high schools sponsor programs that bring in young accident victims, usually in wheelchairs, to show teens what happened to them when they drove irresponsibly. If this isn't available in your community, consider volunteer work with victims of car-related accidents at your local hospital—and on other wards too, like an oncology unit or head-injury ward.

"Seeing how stupid everyone looks doesn't make me want to drink. When I see kids drinking, I think, Why would I want to go out and get so dumb?"
—18-year-old editorial board member

56. Help Her Question the Popularity Puzzle

Helping your daughter resist the pressure and desire to be popular at any price goes hand in hand with helping her resist risky behaviors by showing her what the consequences of those behaviors can be.

When you're a teen and a good part of your world revolves around school and the people you know there, popularity can become very important. Having friends, being well liked, participating in a group: these are all important aspects of being happy and productive. But giving up your true self to achieve that kind of popularity does not promote "Girl Power!" and the assertive, independent spirit the term is meant to encourage. Girls who are able to detach themselves from *needing* to be a part of the in-crowd will be more able to make intelligent choices about what is best for them.

Girls say parents who give them a reality check about popularity can influence their thinking and behavior. Question the prevailing concept of who is popular. One girl said her mother asked her all through middle and high school, "What's different or better about them than anyone else?" The upshot for her was that she treated everyone pretty much the same and ended up well liked by everyone, though not a member of what she called the "in-crowd."

Talk about kids you went to school with and what happened to them later. Let them see high-school popularity is fleeting. One girl talked about meeting some of the people her mother went to high school with who had been very popular then, but who were "losers" later in life. Take your daughter to reunion picnics and talk freely with her afterwards about the people she's met. Sometimes the dorks and wallflowers who went around with their noses in a textbook end up blossoming with interesting careers and lives.

Joining the club (Activity No. 32) can also be a powerful antidote to "popularity pressure." One girl described how her peers teased her when they found out she was a Girl Scout, implying she was a "goody-two-shoes." She didn't care; she thought about all the neat things she had done with her troop that they had not, like earning the money for a Caribbean cruise and traveling to Canada.

"My mom always questioned me when I talked about the 'popular' kids. Like, popular with who? Or what is so great about them that you don't have or can't do? It really helped me think about it and not care as much."
—18-year-old editorial board member

"Teach girls that they are beautiful, smart, independent women, and if people don't like them for that then it is not worth being that person's friend."
—17-year-old survey respondent

WHEN YOUR DAUGHTER REACHES PUBERTY:
SPECIAL CONCERNS AND SUGGESTIONS

57. Take Her Claims of Sexual Harassment and Sexism Seriously

I was surprised by the number of girls who said boys harassed them at school with suggestive comments and discussions of sex and women's bodies within earshot, and male teachers who made sexist and suggestive comments in class.

> There's a lot of evidence that this pattern is widespread. The American Association of University Women (AAUW), in a national study of over 1,600 students, found that 85 percent of the girls surveyed said they had experienced sexual harassment in school.

When girls feel put down or embarrassed or don't really under-stand what is going on, they're quick to blame themselves. Helping girls who are victims of harassment understand what is happening and letting them know that they are not alone can go a long way toward relieving them of guilt and confusion. Many girls say they have just learned to live with it and prefer to get on with their lives rather than be dragged into something they may not be able to handle. This familiar refrain can also be heard by women in the workforce. When I asked girls if they wanted their parents to inter-vene, the answer was generally no, unless the harassment was intol-erable or particularly difficult.

Even if your daughter does not want you to intervene, you can strengthen her by accepting her experiences, helping her understand what harassment is, and equipping her to handle and avoid it. Learn about harassment issues together. Read newspaper articles about leg-islation and court cases. Follow important cases in the media. Dis-cuss what's going on and how you feel about it.

> For help in understanding and preventing harassment, *Sexual Harassment: A Question of Power* will be helpful. For more infor-mation about these books see the "Staying Safe and in Control" resource listings on page 188.

58. Encourage Group Dates

There's an interesting phenomenon developing—the group date—that bodes well for girls in lots of ways.

A group date is one in which a small group goes out, but people are not necessarily paired off. Some might be, while others are not. Girls describe these experiences as "more fun, comfortable, and re-laxed" than the old-fashioned one-on-one date.

Kids may have worked it out that someone they know invited someone they're interested in, and it gives them a chance to be around the object of their curiosity without pressure. Girls say they can be assertive more easily in these situations; there's no guy or date to defer to.

You can foster this activity by suggesting it if it's not occurring in your daughter's circle of friends, offering a place for teens to get together in small groups, and providing transportation.

In a three-year study of factors influencing girls' decisions to be sexually active, Girls Incorporated found that having a steady boyfriend correlated with being sexually active, while high educational aspirations and long-term participation in Girls Incorporated's pregnancy prevention program (Will Power/Won't Power) correlated with a reduced incidence of intercourse. For more information about Girls Incorporated see page 176.

59. Celebrate the No-Date

There was a time when girls wouldn't go to parties or similar social events alone or with other girls. Being dateless was an embarrassment. It meant no one wanted you. No more! Girls are going out without dates, sometimes alone, sometimes with girl buddies. For girls who are doing this, the phenomenon is an exciting reflection of their self-confidence and feelings of self-worth. They don't need a guy to make them feel worthwhile. Girls on my editorial board talked about the fun they had going to their graduating senior prom dateless. The prom became their own celebration on their own terms of themselves and their passage out of high school. They did what they wanted, danced with the partners they wanted to, and left when they wanted to.

The issue of going to events alone dogs the heels of many adult women. What a shame to be missing something interesting or fun simply because we don't want to attend by ourselves. Maybe there's a new generation of girls coming up who won't miss out for this reason. Every parent should applaud, encourage, and celebrate any daughter who wants to go out on a "no-date."

"I had a date for one prom and went to another school's prom with a girlfriend. We got all dressed up and it was really fun. We didn't have to worry about a date. We talked to everyone and danced with whoever we wanted to."
— 18-year-old editorial board member

60. Get Defensive!

For girls, getting defensive means planning ahead to avoid situations that put them at risk, and feeling prepared to deal with a situation that becomes threatening.

Self-defense training can play an important role in helping your daughter, especially girls who are starting to date, feel strong and capable. Knowing how to slow down attackers or disable them can mean the difference between becoming a victim and escaping. In addition, girls who are confident and strong convey an image that doesn't invite attack. Let your daughter know you'll pay for a self-defense class if she wants to enroll, or consider enrolling with her. In addition to the exercise and camaraderie it will foster, it will open the door to discussions of safety and related subjects, like safe dating. Specially designed classes for women and girls will introduce these topics as part of the training. Continue the discussion at an ice-cream shop or coffeehouse after class.

> Look into specialized self-defense programs for girls and women, like the ones offered by Model Mugging (see page 192 in the "Staying Safe and in Control" resource listings).

Avoiding situations that might be risky is certainly one of the best ways to reduce the possibility of attack or assault, but keep in mind that as many as two-thirds of rape cases involve an assailant who was known by the victim. Still, girls can develop strategies—like the "group date" and "no-date" activities suggested in Activities No. 58 and 59—that give them a good measure of control over their environment. Girls who socialize in groups, double date, and go to

> There are lots of good books for girls about staying safe in a risky world, like *The Get Prepared Library of Violence Prevention for Young Women* and *Girl Power: Making Choices and Taking Control*. For more information about these books, and others, check out the "Staying Safe and in Control" resource listings beginning on page 188.

public spots with their dates not only are at less risk for rape or other crimes perpetrated by a third party in isolated locations, they say they act more assertively and feel more in control.

"Karate was one of the greatest things that helped me gain confidence and stand up for myself. In addition to actually building self-defense, it also built self-confidence that I could achieve a lot even if I am a girl."
—16-year-old survey respondent

"Feeling strong about myself and knowing what I want is self-defense from the inside out. Seeing my mom say no to things has helped me stand up for myself."
—18-year-old advisory board member

61. Study the Signs of Pressure and Abuse

Despite group dates, no-dates, and other forms of more inclusive socializing, the day will probably come when your daughter does find someone special with whom she wants to spend time alone.

Prepare her to understand the dynamics of romantic involvements by openly discussing the signs of respectful relationships—and their flip side, ones in which one person is more in control than the other. Television shows, movies, and books can all provide a point of departure for these conversations. How are women treated in their relationships, marriages, at work, or on dates? In movies that feature a young adult or teen romance, talk about how the protagonists treat each other. Is the girl treated respectfully, or is she emotionally abused by being humiliated, condescended to, or deliberately confused? Is she physically or sexually abused? Clip newspaper articles about abuse or sexual violence and use them as a

Books like *Dating Violence: Young Women in Danger* and other books by this author, Barrie Levy, described on page 189 in the "Staying Safe and in Control" resource listings, will provide a good basis for discussion and specific tips and ideas for helping girls recognize warning signs of potentially dangerous relationships.

catalyst for conversations. Volunteer at a shelter for abused women; volunteers are usually required to go through a training session in which statistics about abuse, patterns of behavior, and underlying causes are studied.

"Parents need to let their daughters practice saying no, to stand up for themselves and say they don't want to do something they're not comfortable with. Even if it's something the parents want her to do."
 —18-year-old advisory board member

"Don't give her too much freedom, but don't keep her caged up at home. When she goes somewhere, make sure she knows the rules. Where? With whom? How long? Be aware of dangerous situations, like parties. Are there going to be adults there? Do you know them? Get involved with her life. Invite her friends and their parents over to get to know them."
 —16-year-old survey respondent

Her Body, Her Self

According to a *Glamour* magazine reader survey, 75 percent of American women feel fat. Only 25 percent are. These feelings start early. Twenty to 30 percent of fourth- and fifth-grade girls are concerned about their weight and are dieting. The percentage jumps to 30 to 50 percent by the age of fourteen, and by the time girls are in high school as many as 60 percent of teenage girls are dieting at any given moment.

These statistics shouldn't surprise anyone. The media surrounds us with role models of women and girls who are deathly thin. In *Reviving Ophelia*, Mary Pipher describes how young girls "compare their bodies to our cultural ideals and find them wanting." Puberty for girls has become synonymous with dieting and dissatisfaction with body shape. To achieve our unnaturally thin cultural ideal, girls do unnatural things to their bodies. Some restrict food intake dangerously or overindulge and then induce vomiting. Some do nothing dangerous, but feel ashamed or embarrassed about their bodies and stop engaging in activities where their bodies will be noticed.

Girls' perceptions of their bodies carry over into every aspect of their lives. Girls on my advisory board found that we could not exhaust the topic of body image in our discussions. It is a pervasive issue that erodes every aspect of teen girls' lives and their ability to accept and feel good about themselves.

Despite the increasing number of teen girls with eating disorders and continuing unrealistic role models in the media, there are ways to fight back. This chapter will guide parents through the dangerous terrain of adolescent body image with practical ideas that have helped teenage girls build a positive body image and avoid eating disorders. For example, girls who participate in sports have higher-than-average self-esteem and experience less depression than girls who do not. On another front, girls who understand the physiology of weight gain at puberty and interact with women who appreciate and accept their own bodies are more able to resist media messages glorifying un-realistically thin women and girls.

In addition to these kinds of everyday activities, this chapter will also steer you to resources that can help you tune into, and intervene in, emerging eating disorders and body-image difficulties.

62. Let Her Know Healthy, Not Hot, Is What Counts

No one could say it better than this survey participant: "Being self-conscious about my body is a continual challenge for me, but one that I have basically overcome through exercise, eating well, spiritual self-awareness, and acceptance. By exercising and eating well, I have realized it is more important to have a healthy body than a 'hot' body." This idea is first on the list so it can serve as a beacon for all the other activities, ideas, and resources described in this chapter. In subtle and painfully overt ways our culture communicates to girls that what is going on outside is what counts. Our culture says the most important quality of women is how they look, not what they do, think, or feel.

Do whatever you can not to reinforce this message. Emphasize the importance of feeling healthy, not of looking good. Talk with your daughter about how it feels to be in your body and ask her about her experience of her own body. Talk about things from the inside out. How does it feel during and after exercising? What kinds of exercise feel the best? Why? Is she eating something she enjoys, all the while saying "I shouldn't"? How does she feel after eating too many sweets? How about after a week of good healthy meals? Who are some women she admires and thinks are beautiful because of who they are, not how they look? Start a scrapbook of articles about admirable girls and women based on accomplish-ments, not appearance.

"What has helped me was that all the women I know are normal looking and not super thin or super glamorous, so I always felt comfortable with my looks."
—17-year-old survey respondent

63. Tell Your Daughter She Is Beautiful

When this cropped up again and again in survey responses, I was surprised. On the one hand, girls are struggling to overcome unrealistic stereotypes of our society's ideas about beauty. At the same time they want to be told they're beautiful.

For them, it doesn't mean "You look good." It means you are a neat, radiant person and I can see how interesting and wonderful you are just by looking at you. Girls want the people who are important in their lives to appreciate them and see them as beautiful, no matter how they measure up against society's beauty ruler. Let your daughter know you love the way she looks. Say it out loud and say it over and over again. Let her know you cherish her.

Girls are painfully aware of just how unreal our culture's definition of the ideal female body is. They want to hear from people they love and respect that they are accepted just the way they are. Girls say they especially want to hear their mothers tell them they are beautiful.

"My mother and I have always been really close. A really good piece of advice for moms is to always remind daughters of how good they're doing and how beautiful they are."
—18-year-old survey respondent

"Girls want to know that their parents accept them and think they're beautiful. Moms especially should tell their daughters they're beautiful."
—18-year-old advisory board member

64. Tell Her You're Proud of Her

As important as it is to tell your daughter she is beautiful, let her know you also value her for who she is. Not for what she looks like, or for specific accomplishments, but just because she is who she is.

In a culture in which women receive recognition for how they look, regardless of other qualities or accomplishments, girls want to feel accepted and appreciated just for being. Self-conscious about their bodies and often uncomfortable in them, girls want to know that this encompassing aspect of their lives—their bodies and the changes they're going through—is not on others' minds as much as it is on their own.

"Sometimes when I come home, my mom just tells me she's proud of me. Not for anything special I've done, but just for how I am generally, I guess. It means a lot to me when she says that."
—18-year-old editorial board member

65. Talk with Her about Her Changing Body

At a time when girls are becoming more self-conscious anyway, nature deals them a double whammy in the form of a changing body that's getting fuller and rounder. As their own bodies are naturally filling out, they are becoming more aware of the emaciated feminine "ideal" of today's models, shown in media images.

Help your daughter understand and accept herself and her changing body by talking with her about what is happening. Some of the most obvious things may be puzzles to her. In *What's Happening to My Body*, author Lynda Madaras talks about how some girls don't even realize that growing pubic hair is natural. Don't leave your daughter in the dark. Talk with her and provide her with books about puberty and related topics.

Get your daughter a copy of *What's Happening to My Body* and *My Body, My Self for Girls: The "What's Happening to My Body?" Workbook* that will help her understand and feel good about being a girl. *What's Happening to My Body: A Growing Up Guide for Mothers and Daughters* is a good resource for mothers and daughters to use together. (For information about these books and others, see the resource listing "Body Image and Media Representation of Women" on page 140.)

"I've learned that my hips are a sign that I'm a woman. People shouldn't feel they need to be thin. I've often felt that I could weigh less, but I felt comfortable with myself, and that's enough."
—18-year-old survey respondent

"I was always a really skinny tall girl. Once adolescence hit, I filled out. At first I freaked out, but I know it's normal and exercising has helped me feel good about my body."
—18-year-old survey respondent

66. Examine Body Image in the Media

Examine how body image and beauty are portrayed in the media. Discuss the body images and types you see up on the screen and in the pages of magazines. Spend a couple of hours at the library with a stack of magazines for men and women. Do a count of how many articles there are in each that discuss physical appearance and dieting. And for the women's magazines, compare the number of diet articles and recipes that sit side by side. Talk about how the two of you feel when you see unrealistically thin women held up as the ideal. Hopeless? Helpless? Angry?

Get rid of magazines and other material in your house that contribute to the helpless, hopeless, angry feelings. Seek out images of women and girls that emphasize accomplishments and smarts. The girls' magazines listed on page 172 are full of healthy diverse images of girls. The list of "Books about Good Books for Girls" (page 130) is another good resource for finding role models of women and girls who are smart, resourceful individuals whose lives don't revolve around how they look.

"Whenever my family watched TV and one of those I haven't-eaten-for-the-past-three-months-and-that's-why-I'm-so-skinny models would come on, my parents always said something like, 'It's not healthy to be that skinny.' This was reinforced all the time."
　—18-year-old survey respondent

"Many girls are self-conscious about their bodies because of various magazines like Seventeen. *But those dreams are unrealistic."*
　—17-year-old survey respondent

Want to find out who some of the worst offenders in advertising are? Or buy a poster, button, or T-shirt protesting how women are portrayed? Visit About-Face, founders of the Stop Starvation Imagery Campaign, at www.about-face.org. For more information on About-Face and other organizations, like Media Watch and WINS (Women Insisting On Natural Shapes), see page 146.

67. Investigate and Celebrate How Women Look

Only in this century and in our media-driven global culture has the "idealized" image of women been one that would have women be emaciated and sexually undeveloped. Historically, and in many contemporary cultures, a more rounded body image is accepted as natural and beautiful.

Wander through history and into other cultures with your daughter to get a more diverse picture of the acceptable range of women's body types. Visit your local library together and check out

A great book to stimulate discussion between mothers and daughters about beauty is *I Am Beautiful: A Celebration of Women in Their Own Words* (see page 141).

art history and anthropology books. Get books of art from other cultures and countries, like India and tribal African groups. They'll offer a smorgasbord of alternatives to the narrow range of women we see in the media.

"In seventh grade, I took a social action class that contributed to my healthy body image. One of the things we studied was a cross-cultural comparison of women's body image and then a historical evolution of women's body image in our culture. I learned that it's just a cultural phase and that it could easily change."
—17-year-old survey respondent

"One thing that has helped me maintain a healthy body image is knowing that everyone is different, and that every culture has a different image of a perfect body. I stay in shape with sports, but even through that I was unsatisfied with my body sometimes because somebody always has a better body. But soon I realized that my body was really good the way it is."
—18-year-old survey respondent

68. Research Your Family Body Types

Along with knowing that women come in all shapes and sizes, girls find liberation when they see firsthand the effect genes have on their weight and size. Understanding the connection, and moving toward acceptance and appreciation as a result, doesn't take a serious scientific inquiry. You may have all the evidence you need in an old shoe box or packed away in the closet.

If you have a family album of your parents and their siblings, pull it out. Do you have pictures of yourself when you were a teen? Spread them all out and take a look at them with your daughter. Talk about similarities and differences in appearance, including height and body types. Are most people long skinny drinks of water, or solid-looking wrestler types? Does your daughter look a lot like you, or more like the other side of the family? Talk about any fondness you have for individuals that is related to their appearance. Was your father's brother a bear-like uncle who could twirl two kids in the air without even feeling it? Was your skinny cousin always the one to shimmy down behind the furniture to retrieve missing toys because no one else could fit?

Also talk about positive qualities unrelated to appearance. The uncle who twirled you in the air was also the uncle who always took the time to ask you how school was going. And, here's the grandmother who told the best bedtime stories you've ever heard.

As you look at this photo gallery of the family genes, talk about the thoughts and feelings that come up. Encourage your daughter to accept and celebrate her place in this cast of interesting characters.

"When I see models that are size one and five-ten it really makes me feel that I shouldn't worry about my weight, and anyway people in my family just aren't very skinny."
—17-year-old survey respondent

69. Don't Tease Her About Her Changing Appearance

At an age when girls are trying to figure out who they are, their bodies start changing on them! And to make things worse, they often get teased about their changing bodies.

At this sensitive, confusing time, even an innocent comment on an adult's part can be interpreted as a criticism. Comments like "You're really filling out and turning into a young woman," or "You're going to need new sweaters if you keep growing like that," only add to the confusion. These kinds of comments may be intended on your part as acknowledgment of the fact that she is growing up. Unfortunately, the filling out that accompanies growing up has become a form of betrayal to many girls who wish they still had their thin tomboyish bodies.

Stick to acknowledging her as a person and recognizing her choices as a maturing young woman. Tell her she's beautiful as suggested in Activity No. 63, and let her know you're proud of her. If you make comments about her appearance, compliment her choice of clothes in ways that emphasize something special about her, like her artistic flair or sense of fun, rather than only how she looks.

"Fathers should never make fun of or tease their daughters about the way they look. Say only positive things!"
—18-year-old survey respondent

Celebrating Girls has some great insights and suggestions for helping your daughter as her focus shifts to increased awareness of, and interest in, her appearance. (See the listings of "Books for Girls" on page 125 for more information about *Celebrating Girls*.)

70. Set an Example

Many of the girls who report accepting and feeling good about their bodies, eating well, and exercising regularly talked about how their parents set a good example. For many, it was not something they thought about much or realized until they started taking health classes or learning about nutrition and other related health issues. They just picked up the attitudes and behaviors as they were growing up. They're glad they did, though, and appreciate that they have fewer food and body-image struggles than many of their peers.

If you aren't nutrition savvy and don't exercise much, get started. It's good for you and good for your daughter. (The next few activity ideas can get you started.)

One caveat girls mentioned in this context is an exaggerated focus on external appearance. Eating well and exercising should be about feeling good, energetic, and healthy, not about being beautiful.

"I always ate a lot of balanced meals when I was growing up because nutrition was important to my mom. And playing tennis and soccer helped me maintain a healthy body."
—16-year-old survey respondent

If mothers want to understand just how much they influence their daughters' eating patterns and body image, take a look at *Like Mother, Like Daughter: How Women Are Influenced by Their Mothers' Relationship with Food—and How to Break the Pattern* (see page 141). This book also includes great practical suggestions for healthy eating and exercise.

71. Junk the Junk Food

Even girls who know junk food is full of fat and sugar have trouble avoiding it when they're surrounded by it. Keeping it out of the house helps. If you and your daughter are not very nutrition or junk-food savvy, research the issues together. As you're digging up information, focus on foods and menus that are healthy, rather than on diets and calorie counting.

A fun Web site to visit that will motivate you to steer clear of junk food, or at least pick the healthiest options, is www.olen.com/food, where you can call up any fast-food restaurant and request nutritional data on their menus. (Olen.com is sponsored by Olen Publishing, who publishes *Fast Food Facts* developed by the Minnesota Attorney General's office.) An important caveat on this point relates to Activity No. 73 ("Discourage Her from Dieting"): Don't try to control what your daughter eats. If something is taboo, rest assured your daughter will want it. Nor will she be immune to advertising and wanting what her peers eat—as do adults. Junking the junk food is not about control; it is about role models, habits, and opportunities. Recognize that within the sane environment you set up, your daughter will still probably want to participate in the food culture of her peers. It's more important to set the stage for self-regulation than to attempt to control every calorie or fat gram she eats.

"I exercise regularly and feel good about my body, but my mom does not buy junk food. We eat a lot of fruits and vegetables."
—16-year-old survey respondent

"My mom has always encouraged my sisters, brother, and me to be physically active and she didn't allow junk food or developing unhealthy eating habits, so we naturally eat healthier than most kids and don't really gain weight."
—16-year-old survey respondent

72. Hold "Good Food" Days

For girls (and women) who are dissatisfied with their weight and their bodies, food is an enemy. Make it a friend. You can eat healthy food abundantly. Make "Good Food Days" a fun event by researching and planning a healthy menu. Try something you've never had before. Check out ethnic foods, often prepared with fresh ingredients and complex carbohydrates, like corn or bulgur, which are healthy and filling. Shop for needed ingredients with your daughter—and shopping for ingredients for ethnic dishes may turn into an adventure of its own. Then cook up a storm, and enjoy a great meal together. This might be one of those meals the two of you enjoy alone (and that girls say they especially want to share with their mothers), or it might be something you share with family and friends.

> Check out *Jane Brody's Good Food Book* (Jane Brody, Doubleday) for lots of ideas about how to prepare interesting wholesome foods. Nutritionist Brody also has other books in this series, like *Jane Brody's Good Seafood Book,* that will help bring variety to your efforts.

73. Discourage Her from Dieting

Chronic dieters know that diets don't work. In *Like Mother, Like Daughter,* nutritionist Debra Waterhouse asks, Why, if Weight Watchers is so effective, do women return time after time?

Teen dieting can start a lifelong pattern of disordered eating and a body that conserves fat cells. When calories are restricted, the body does a smart thing in evolutionary terms: it conserves fat and burns muscle. Since fat has more calories than muscle, your body protects you from a possible calorie shortage by conserving fat to burn during a food shortage. The problem is that your daughter is not going to face a food shortage. She's just going to reduce her muscle mass, lower her metabolism, and *improve* her fat cells' storage capacity, only making weight loss harder and slower. And ironically for girls and women—but not for men—this phenomenon results in increased fat storage in the hips, buttocks, and thighs—the three fat repositories most universally feared by fat-conscious females.

Diets don't work, anyway. Most people who lose weight by dieting gain it back. And for girls, adding fat at puberty is essential. Body-fat percentage increases at puberty from about 12 percent to about 20 percent to prepare the body for reproductive functions. Restricting calories at this juncture can result in long-term health problems, like reduced bone density. *Like Mother, Like Daughter* (see page 141) offers an excellent discussion of these issues.

By starting your daughter on a path to sensible fitness activities and healthy eating habits, you will have an enormous impact on her life as a teen and an adult.

Encourage your daughter to use a safe, healthy approach to getting fit and losing weight (if her physician says it's safe for her to do so) by giving her helpful resources. *The Right Moves: A Girl's Guide to Getting Fit and Feeling Good* and Debra Waterhouse's workbook, based on principles from *Like Mother, Like Daughter*, are great places to start. (Information about these books is included in the resource listings in "Body Image and Media Representation of Women" on page 140.)

If you think your daughter has or is headed for an eating disorder, there is help. Contact the National Eating Disorders Organization (NEDO), which can provide guidance and referrals. (See page 145 for more information about NEDO.)

"I was the same way [dissatisfied with my body], but I love to run so I tried out for track and field. I ran and had fun, and I also lost weight."
—15-year-old survey respondent

74. Join the No-Diet Day Celebration

May sixth is official International No-Diet Day, when people of all sizes join together to say they've heard and seen enough of the obsession with thinness and dieting. It's a time to celebrate size and shape diversity with walkathons, workshops, and panel discussions. All these activities are designed to educate people about how the media influences our ideas of beauty, and empower us to transcend artificial and dangerous definitions.

For more information about No Diet Day contact the Council on Size and Weight Discrimination (see page 144). They have an activity packet and a database of groups and individuals who belong to the No-Diet Day Coalition.

"I think every girl should have food celebration days when they stop worrying about dieting and their bodies."
— 18-year-old advisory board member

75. Don't Focus on Weight and Fat

Girls who feel pretty good about their weight and how they look stress that their parents didn't make a big deal about weight. They didn't talk much about their daughter's weight, their own weight, or the weight of friends or strangers. They talked about other attributes that are more important.

It's pretty clear from experts who deal with body image and weight issues that trying to control someone's size—or your own—leads to a focus on weight and food that makes people unhappy. Whether they control their size or not, the lives of people who are overly focused on these issues are ruled by what they eat (or don't eat), how they feel about their size (that day in particular and every day in general), how they think they look, and how they want to look. Spare your daughter this future and don't make weight and fat a driving force in your own life or hers.

"I think the main reason I've managed to maintain a healthy body image is that my parents never implied that there was any importance in it. I have a friend whose mom told her all through childhood and

adolescence that she needed to lose weight and all it did was make her extremely self-conscious."

—18-year-old advisory board member

"Girls should always love their body, because it's theirs and they can't change that."

—16-year-old survey respondent

To help your daughter with the "I feel fat" complaint, get a copy of *When Girls Feel Fat: Helping Girls Through Adolescence.* If you have unresolved weight and body-image issues yourself, they undoubtedly affect your daughter. Check out the book for adults *Full and Fulfilled: The Science of Eating to Your Soul's Satisfaction.* (Information about both books is included in the "Body Image and Media Representation of Women" resource listings on page 140.)

76. Don't Try to Control What She Eats

This may seem like a contradiction to many of the preceding suggestions, but it's not. When you junk the junk food, hold good food days, and learn about nutrition together, you are increasing the odds that your daughter will have the facts, environment, and attitudes she needs to develop a healthy relationship with her own body and with eating. Eating disorders are not really about food; they're about feeling in control. For girls to feel in control of themselves in relation to food, eating needs to be a self-regulated process. To help your daughter become self-regulated, surround her with good food, good role models, good information, and accurate ideas about women's body sizes and types.

If you are concerned that your daughter is developing an unhealthy relationship with food, contact Eating Disorders Awareness and Prevention, Inc. (page 144) and visit the Anorexia Nervosa and Related Eating Disorders Web Site at www.anred.com for background information.

Your daughter will almost certainly indulge in some junk food. Let her. What's important is that she has an opportunity to observe and practice good eating habits, not that she eat perfectly all the time.

"My family was never controlling of how much or how little I ate or even what I ate, which I'm sure has made a huge difference for me [for my body image]."
—18-year-old advisory board member

77. Work up a Sweat Together

Everything from power walking, aerobics classes, and tennis to hiking and more was named by girls as favorite ways to exercise. Try lots of different activities that force you to push yourselves and get your pulses racing. It doesn't matter if you're good at them. What's important is that you and your daughter have fun—and a little trouble breathing. Give her a role model of adults—especially women—who don't mind breaking a sweat and taking on the challenge of a little competition and new activities.

To keep it interesting and fun, make a list of all the things you can do together. What about tennis, handball, or swimming laps? Write down anything that catches your fancy and keep the list for a day when you're in the mood for something new.

Along with the immediate benefits of exercise, there are also long-term benefits to getting your daughter moving. The National Cancer Institute found that three hours of exercise a week from the teen years through age forty can reduce the rate of breast cancer by 20 to 30 percent. Four or more hours can reduce it by almost 60 percent.

"I think it's important to do physically active things with teenage girls so they don't forget what their bodies can do and so they don't feel like the only way for their bodies to have value is to be pretty and skinny. There is more value in being strong and able."
—18-year-old advisory board member

"Nothing makes you feel better in attitude and body than a good work-out!"
—17-year-old survey respondent

78. Share Relaxing Noncompetitive Sports and Physical Activities

In contrast to the break-a-sweat exercise described above, and in spite of girls' increased interest and participation in organized competitive sports, they also want to play without the pressure of competing and the goal of winning. They want to share relaxed physical activities with their families in settings where they know their body and its capabilities will be accepted.

Complement your workouts in Activity No. 77 with a relaxed game of Frisbee or Hacky Sack. Try a leisurely bike ride, or take a hike without the pressure of having to get somewhere. For girls, it's an opportunity to talk and explore, not a time to accomplish a goal.

For fun, noncompetitive activity ideas, check out *The Cooperative Sport and Games Book: Challenge without Competition* (Terry Orlick, Pantheon Books). In a study comparing girls' competitive and cooperative sports participation, researchers found that both types enhanced physical fitness, but cooperative sports also enhanced healthy attitudes about appearance.

"By being exposed to women who were physically active, like my gym teacher and my own mother, I was shown that women could be strong, and that to be strong was good and I could be strong too."
—18-year-old advisory board member

79. Mothers, Accept Compliments

It's hard for a lot of women to accept compliments gracefully. Often their first response to receiving one is to describe why it's not true: why they're not beautiful, what their major flaws are, or why the meal isn't that great, ad infinitum. Professional women who may gracefully accept praise on the job often have more trouble receiving it in personal relationships. This is ironic, since often there is a girl watching—and learning. Learning that women shouldn't feel too good about themselves, think too highly of themselves, or be too bold about just how great they really are. Learn to accept compliments and be a role model for your daughter.

"I realize how important it is for a mother to reflect a positive image to her daughter. The best thing a mother can do for a daughter is to gracefully accept compliments."
—18-year-old survey respondent

80. Give Her a Sporting Chance

Participating in an organized team sport with peers came up again and again as a key for many girls to feeling good about their bodies. The feelings of competence and confidence that develop from playing a team sport help combat the desire so many girls have to fit the emaciated-model mold.

Research shows that getting girls involved as early as possible increases the odds that they'll be involved when they're older, but it's never too late. A surprising number of girls who completed the survey for this book said they didn't start participating in sports until their teens and plan to continue indefinitely. Once they experience the camaraderie and physical and psychological benefits, they don't want to stop!

> Girls who are active in sports and recreational activities feel greater confidence, self-esteem, and pride in their physical and social selves than do kids who are sedentary.

> In a *Psychology Today* study, women whose primary motivation for exercising was fitness had better body images than those who exercised to improve their appearance. Foster the idea of sports and exercise as a way to get fit, not as a means to a great-looking body.

"Getting into sports and seeing that girls come in all shapes and sizes was good for me. I was into dieting and trying to be a size one. But when I started playing field hockey, I decided if my body was healthy then it must look great."
—16-year-old survey respondent

"I participated in competitive swimming and it helped me maintain a healthy body image. I was a chubby kid up to age ten, when I began to swim. If I had continued my same eating habits without the benefit of swimming, I would have been an unhappy teenager worried about her weight."
—17-year-old survey respondent

81. Encourage Her to Push Her Physical Limits

Distinct from organized sports, pushing limits means different things for different girls. For girls who are already athletic or physically active, it may mean seeking out special opportunities like sports camps, where they can play with and against other top-notch girl athletes. It might mean a rock-climbing class or an Outward Bound adventure with other teens. For girls who feel clumsy or think of themselves as "klutzes" (their word), it might mean a daily walk around the neighborhood at a brisk pace. If that's the case, do it together. One daughter and her mother have been taking a twenty-minute walk almost daily for years. It not only gets their blood going, but it has helped them stay in touch despite busy schedules.

For girls with physical limitations, pushing their limits may mean participating in specialized activities where they can interact with others at their own level. (For help in finding a camp for girls with special needs, visit www.kidscamps.com.)

Moving is healthy. Help your daughter find *her* activity and *her* difficulty level, and then encourage, participate, and provide resources.

"Camp Esperanza [for young people with arthritis] made me feel like I was a whole person again because I met other kids who had similar health problems, as well as adults who grew up successfully with their

disease. We were also challenged to participate safely in strenuous phys-ical and group cooperative exercises."

   —20-year-old survey respondent

"An important activity that contributed to my confidence and self-esteem was weight lifting in my gym class. All the boys and some of the girls told me not to do it because it was for boys. I wanted to show them that nothing was just for boys and even though I was in a lot of pain at first, I stuck with it and got a B."

   —15-year-old survey respondent

In studies of girls and women, weight training and strength train-ing have been found to improve participants' concept of their physical abilities and their appearance. Noncompetitive training experiences in which girls participated in small groups, rather than competing as individuals, contributed to improved self-concept the most.

For information about camps for girls, visit www.femina.com (page 154), where you'll find a list of resources for girls, including specialized camps. Also consider a planned adventure with your daughter, like the ones offered by Woodswomen. You can pick the level of challenge and the type of activity, from hiking to sail-ing and just about everything in between. For more information, see page 186.

What Can She Be?

What can she be? She can be confident, self-reliant, and economically self-sufficient.

What does it take for a teenage girl to grow into a confident, self-reliant, and self-sufficient woman? First, girls need to know that being smart is cool. That having big dreams is hot. That earning, understanding, and managing their own money are keys to having control over their futures. That education increases their choices and earning potential. That math, science, and high-tech skills aren't just for nerds and guys.

One survey participant learned many of the lessons promoted in this chapter when her parents divorced: "There's never been a question in my mind as to what a female can or cannot do. I learned this from watching my mother after my parents' divorce. It was just my mom and me on our own. She worked so hard to make sure I had a comfortable lifestyle. Watching all the stuff she went through puts no limits in my mind of what females can do. She has helped me develop the dream of accomplishing anything I really want."

The suggestions in this chapter will help your daughter dream big and develop the skills she'll need to support her dreams. They'll help her feel smart and act smart. They'll encourage her to explore the world of work; to participate in math, science, and high-tech activities; to handle money and use it as a means toward an end; and to think about the future and how to create one filled with opportunity and satisfaction.

82. Praise Brains and Competence

Girls are bombarded with images in movies and magazines and on television shows that glorify women for their looks and compliance, not for their brains or ability to get things done. In *School Girls: Young Women, Self-Esteem and the Confidence Gap* (see page 167), Peggy Orenstein describes girls who underachieve in math and pass on answering questions in class because they don't want boys to know they're smart.

Let your daughter know that being smart isn't just good, it's great. Smart means being thoughtful, using critical-thinking skills, analyzing situations, and taking action to influence events. From this combination of good thinking and action flows competence.

Watch the little things your daughter does and tell her how smart she was to handle something a certain way. Was she a genius at getting her younger brother to clean up by making it into a game? Did she figure out how to change the flat tire on her bike? Did she calculate how long it would take to get to camp by car? Don't let these natural displays of intelligence go unnoticed.

Seek out situations where she can excel, whether it's a sports camp, a Saturday writers' workshop, volunteering with younger girls, or pushing herself to take college-placement math. Be impressed with, and curious about, what she's doing. Ask lots of questions and respond a lot with "Wow." Girls say they're embarrassed by receiving praise, but acknowledge that they love it, especially from important people in their lives.

Along with noticing and praising your daughter, notice and praise her peers and women in the news who model brains and competence. Talk about what they're saying and doing, not what they're wearing. Show her a world populated by bright women who are rewarded for their brains and competence and encourage her to become one of them.

"I think the most important thing that helped me stay strong and intelligent was my parents' encouragement. They never praised weakness or stupidity, but celebrated strength and intelligence."
—17-year-old survey respondent

"My father always asked me intelligent questions and never underesti-mated my ability to understand. He never said, 'You'll get it when you're older.' He just explained it to me because he felt I deserved to know the answer."
— 17-year-old survery respondent

83. Brag About Her Accomplishments

Did your daughter just go to the state track meet? Get a new job or start visiting seniors in convalescent homes? Maybe she got a great report card, or planned and pulled off her little sister's birthday party.

When you introduce your daughter to friends or co-workers, let them know this is "the math whiz who just aced her calculus exam," "the middle-schooler who started a recycling program at her school," or "the literature-lover who's going to a camp for young writers." Your daughter will know you are proud of her and, as important or even more important, she will get the message that what she does in the world matters.

Don't turn the bragging into teasing or a situation that draws an embarrassing amount of attention. Be proud and matter-of-fact. Much as girls say they like knowing their parents are proud of them, parental bragging is a mixed blessing because it can quickly become embarrassing. Use it in moderation to show respect and admiration.

"I was really surprised when I met some of the people my mom works with. They knew so much about me. It was kind of embarrassing, but it was cool too because I know she's proud of me."
— 18-year-old editorial board member

"Introduce your daughter to your friends and show her you're proud of her and proud that she's your daughter."
— 17-year-old survey respondent

84. Stay in Touch with School Learning

Girls want to know their parents are interested in what they're doing in school. Ask about classes, papers, and special projects. If she needs resources or assistance to complete an assignment, help her figure out what she needs and how she can get it. Talk about homework assignments and set the expectation that homework will always get done. Visit her school, get to know her teachers, and attend extra-curricular events.

In addition to asking and participating, watch for things that might be obstacles to full participation in school. Are boys teasing or harassing girls? Is a teacher not expecting much from them? Are certain extracurricular activities unavailable? One girl, interested in computers, talked about how uncomfortable she was in the computer lab where the mostly boy occupants were unfriendly and talked openly about girls and their bodies within earshot. By talking with school administrators and the computer teacher, this girl and her mother were able to get guidelines established for acceptable lab behavior. *School Girls: Young Women, Self-Esteem and the Confidence Gap* and *Failing at Fairness* (both described in the "Gender Equity, Feminism, and Equal Rights" resource listings on page 163) are useful books that will give you an idea of the kinds of blatant and subtle obstacles your daughter might face.

Talk about education and what it can mean for your daughter's future. Seek out facts about how education can have an effect on her ability to control her financial future and lead a fulfilling life.

> Education does make a difference. U.S. Census Bureau data show that women with some high-school education earn less than $10,000 annually, while women with a high-school diploma average more, but still less than $15,000. Women with a two-year college degree earn an average of $20,000 and women with a four-year degree, $25,000. For women with a master's degree, the average jumps to over $30,000.

"My mom sits down with me and I tell her everything about my school and after-school activities. This has helped me a lot because if I ever had a problem, she always had an answer or suggestion."
—17-year-old survey respondent

"Be cognizant of your daughter's life at school. Ask her how her day was and tell her about yours. Respect her just like you want to be respected."
—16-year-old survey respondent

85. Make Math and Science Fun

When my editorial board talked about their middle-school science classes, their eyes lit up. They described making worm farms and miniature landfills. They gardened and went on astronomy field trips. They were active, problem-solving learners. But when high school started, things changed. Science became more of a sit-in-your-chair-and-learn-from-lectures kind of education experience. The connections to everyday life and opportunities for problem-solving in small groups were eliminated. The appeal and excitement were lost, even for one girl who is a math and science whiz.

In spite of this, there are things you can do to make math and science fun. Seek out learning opportunities for your daughter that give her the chance to work in small groups, have influence over what she learns, and relate math and science learning to subjects she's interested in. Also important is involvement with interested adults who will encourage her to excel. These suggestions are based on the findings of the American Association of University Women reported on in *Growing Smart: What's Working for Girls in School*. And there are lots of ways to create this environment for your daughter to augment good school experiences or ensure ones that will foster math and science participation if her school does not. Check "Organizations" (page 157) in the "Math, Science, and Technology" resource listings for information about interesting programs. Programs like Equals and the Math Science Network, which are offered in many locations around the country, use an interactive, real-world approach to foster girls' interest in these subjects. Also check out Advocates for Women in Science, Engineering and Mathematics for information about women scientists serving as mentors for girls interested in science careers. Science-By-Mail uses a model that fits the criteria described by the American Association of University Women, and you and your daughter can initiate the program from home. Look into programs like Cool Science and Technology Badges, sponsored by the Girl Scouts, and Operation SMART, sponsored by Girls Incorporated. (For information about these organizations see pages 176 and 178 in the "National Organizations" resource listings.) Also let your daughter know that being a scientist, or having a technical bent, can be neat. *Twentieth-Century Women Scientists* (page 153) and *Girls and Young Women Inventing* (page

152) are some good books to get started with, and a visit to the International Women's Air and Space Museum's Web site (page 159) and www.awsem.org will show girls that being a woman scientist is cool and offers opportunities to do interesting and exciting things.

As skills that open doors to many work opportunities and good-paying jobs, math and science are important in their own right, but competence in them is also important for girls' development. Girls who enjoy and perform well in math and science report more positive feelings about schoolwork, career aspirations, and overall self-esteem than do girls who do not perform well. (See page 175 about the American Association of University Women, whose report *How Schools Shortchange Girls* looked at these and related issues).

"They say science is for nerds and 'pocket protector' people, but I don't fit into any of those categories. Right now I have a project in an international science and engineering fair and when people say I'm going to 'Nerd Fest,' I simply smile and say I'm looking forward to the adventure and competition with people from thirty-three countries."
—18-year-old survey respondent

"Be impressed if your daughter is good in math and science. It's not okay to tell her it's okay if she's not."
—18-year-old advisory board member

"I joined lots of clubs, including the traditional 'boys' clubs' in math and science that involve critical thinking. There were rarely any girls in these clubs and I was determined to break the barrier. Being in 'their club' made me feel good because I proved to them I was just as good as them and could compete."
—20-year-old survey respondent

86. Get Her Wired

Computer competence is becoming standard fare for jobs at all levels, from administrative support roles to top management from creative types in the arts to technical specialists. In addition, with Internet connections and E-mail, computers will be a standard household appliance of the twenty-first century.

Girls who are already wired and comfortable with computers love it and know they have a leg up in the job market. Most girls who haven't taken the plunge because they don't have the resources or are afraid of computers know they need to overcome these obstacles and get involved.

Research shows that girls and women see computers primarily as a tool for accomplishing an end. Boys, on the other hand, love them as toys and fiddle around with them just for the fun of it. As a result, they often become more experienced with how computers work and more comfortable with them. This confidence and competence lead naturally to jobs that are in demand and pay well, like programming and hardware support.

For more information about the issues involved in fostering girls' computer literacy, take a look at *Does Jane Compute?* (see page 152). You'll find lots of good ideas about how to get them involved, along with information that will convince you to get your daughter wired.

To get started, take your cue from the research; offer computer-based experiences that allow your daughter to pursue her interests and hobbies. Does she like to write? Look into an electronic journal. Is she a budding artist? Try one of many fun, easy-to-use painting or drawing programs. Is she curious about other cultures? Get her started with an E-mail pen pal from across the globe. Is she doing something innovative or interesting, like starting a recycling program at school? Encourage her to set up a Web site to let other teens know about her work. If you don't have a computer, make it a priority to budget for one. Until you do have one, check your local library; many now have Internet rooms where people can sign up to use a computer for a certain amount of time. Take the list of girls' Web sites that starts on page 153 in the resource listings and surf the Web with your daughter. (Many of these sites also offer free E-mail and Web site space for girls.) Encourage her to use the Internet to do research for school work as well as for other projects (like learning about a good summer camp).

To use technology, you don't need to be a scientist, mathematician, or technology buff. And while it's important to open the doors for girls to the exciting world of math, science, and technology as careers, it's equally important to let them know that skills in these areas can also be tools for pursuing other interests and careers. Being comfortable with a computer is as important in today's work world for non-techie types like journalists and graphic designers as it is for scientists.

In its 1998 report, *Gender Gaps: Where Schools Still Fail Our Children*, the American Association of University Women found girls are catching up in math and science, but still fall behind boys in computer use. Not only do girls use computers less than boys do, they use often use them for relatively low-level activities like sending E-mail and word processing. Keyboard comfort is important, but it is not enough. Encourage your daughter to program or animate a game, design a Web site, or set up a database for her club. To give her lots of role models and ideas about just how cool a computer career can be, check out *Cool Careers for Girls in Computers* (see page 151).

"I use my computer for everything. I do research, plan trips with maps and restaurants, buy airplane tickets, work on school papers. People need to get their kids involved!"
—18-year-old editorial board member

"My freshman year in high school, I was one of three girls in a computer class of about thirty. I enrolled in the class with an interest in creating a CD-ROM that would teach sign language to deaf and hearing students. I enjoyed working on the CD-ROM, but much of my daily learning was about gender inequity. The computer lab was a very loud, competitive environment where boys one-upped one another with the newest software, hardware, and computer tricks. This environment worked to create an atmosphere of intimidation for many girls who are

not raised in a culture that encourages them to be computer savvy. Girls need a comfortable place to use and learn computers to find out what a creative and powerful tool they can be."
—18-year-old advisory board member

87. Incorporate the Arts

Young girls and boys both like art activities. Preschoolers love to play music, cut, color, paste, and paint. And it's a good thing they do. Early childhood educators emphasize that these experiences lay a foundation for later, more complex visual and mathematical thinking.

Many boys drop out of these activities when they move into elementary school, but girls often continue. If your daughter still enjoys art activities, crafts, and music, actively work to keep her involved. That quilt she's designing takes some pretty sophisticated geometry, even if it's not recognized as such. That sculpture she's been working on requires visual thinking skills similar to those required of an industrial engineer.

If she's left her love of art and music behind—particularly if she is a poor performer in math and science—explore ways to reinvolve her. Sponsor a monthly girls' craft morning at your house where your daughter and her friends can socialize and create. If she likes to sew, challenge her with complex patterns or craft items where two-dimensional fabric becomes 3-D soft sculptures. Offer to pay for music lessons, perhaps with an off-beat instrument to pique her interest. Attend concerts and visit museums and art galleries to stimulate her interest. Take a cyber-stroll through the National Museum of Women in the Arts at www.nmwa.org. Visit the girls' Web sites described on page 153 of the resource listings where she can see what other girls are doing in the arts.

It's unfortunate that music and the arts are often the first subjects to get the ax when school cost-cutting measures are taken. Far from

The annual College Board Profile of College Bound Seniors shows that students who have participated in arts education have higher SAT exam scores than do students who have not.

frills, these subjects foster the very thinking skills that are often difficult for students to master. Give your daughter a leg up: Encourage her interest in the arts for their own sake.

"Taking art classes has helped me a lot. I have become an intern for a glass-blowing and stained-glass artist and it has opened new windows and doors in my life."
—17-year-old survey respondent

"I've always liked to draw and my parents always encouraged me. I went to a career fair and found out about a lot of things I could do. One was about architects, and now I think that's what I want to be."
—17-year-old survey respondent

88. Talk About Your Past

Another title for this activity could have been "Talk about Her Future," but many girls said it's easier for them to move into a discussion about themselves by hearing their parents or other adults' stories about their pasts. Not lectures or morality tales, but stories. Interesting, funny, sad, and surprising stories. As one girl said, "Hearing about my parents' past and knowing they were kids once too makes me think about my future."

Talk with your daughter about what you wanted to be when you were young. Talk about the fears you had, and some of the dumb things you did along the way. And some of the smart things you did that turned out well. To a teenager the future looks big, exciting, and often scary. Let her know no one navigates his or her life goals without a slip or tumble along the way. Let her know you've made mistakes and you're still here to talk about it. And let her know that you've had lots of great experiences and that she will too.

Talking about how the world has changed in your lifetime is another way to help your daughter plan for the future. Help her understand that the world of her future will be a different place than it is today. For most adults reading this book, desktop computers either didn't exist when they were growing up or they were an esoteric, hard-to-use appliance that didn't sit in living rooms and dens as they do now. When I mentioned to my editorial board the price of my first home, one girl laughed and said, "You can't buy a good used car for that much these days."

According to an employment data summary by Girls Count, 90 percent of today's kindergarteners will be employed in jobs that do not exist today.

As the conversation moves to your daughter's future—and it will if she feels relaxed and unpressured in your conversations—talk with her about her ideas regarding work, career, finances, and family. The purpose of these conversations shouldn't be to figure it all out, but rather they should be a way for you to let your daughter know her future is an important thing to think about, and for you to begin exploring the issues together.

For guidance in having productive conversations about the future with your daughter, check these books by Mindy Bingham and Sandy Stryker: *Choices: A Young Woman's Guide to Self Awareness and Personal Planning* (see page 126), *Mother-Daughter Choices: A Handbook for the Coordinator* (see page 136), *Things Will Be Different for My Daughter: A Practical Guide to Building Her Self-Esteem and Self-Reliance* (see page 160), and *Career Choices* (see page 138).

"Parents bringing up stupid things they did helps me feel like I'll turn out okay. It makes you think about your goals."
    —18-year-old editorial board member

"One thing my father and I always did was talk about my schooling and my future. Having talks like this gave me more confidence about succeeding at my dreams and goals. My father made me realize that I should focus if I want to succeed."
    —18-year-old survey respondent

89. Become a Goalie

Does your daughter say "I wish . . ." or "I sure would like to . . ." or "I wonder if I'll ever . . ."? If she does—and most girls do—it's the perfect opportunity to help her turn wishes and wants into goals.

Being a goalie is the flip side of talking about the future. Being a goalie is about helping your daughter make her dreamed-for future a reality. The future might be just a few days off; what does she need to do to get all her homework done early so she can go on a weekend camping trip with her friend's family? It might be a summer camp she's interested in attending three months down the road during summer vacation. Or it might be preparation for attending a certain college, years away.

One caveat girls were very definite about: Make sure the goals are your daughter's, not yours. Girls want their parents to be accepting of, and curious about, their interests. Listen carefully to what your daughter says about her dreams and hopes. Notice what she gravitates toward and support those interests. Is your daughter interested in being an environmental biologist? Do you wonder what that even means? Show your daughter you're interested in learning by asking her questions, getting a book on the subject, surfing the Net, or going to a public talk. Surprise her by gathering information for her about ways she can pursue her interests. Buy her a book on her area of interest. Offer to match dollar for dollar anything she earns and uses to pursue her interest. Along with helping her take concrete steps toward reaching her goals—large and small—showing an interest in what she cares about gives her the important message that she matters.

Take a look at *Peterson's Summer Opportunities for Kids and Teenagers* (Ellen Beal, Peterson's Guides). Updated annually, this book includes information about more than 1,800 camps and academic programs on every topic imaginable.

"My mother is very supportive of every activity I'm involved in, but she lets me do my own thing. At times she will back off and let me figure out things for myself. At other times she will lend a helping hand."
—17-year-old survey respondent

"Ask lots of questions about things she's interested in so you can learn more about it and also help her think about it more."
—18-year-old editorial board member

90. Get the Facts on Love, Marriage, and Money

In an era when more and more women work outside the home out of economic necessity, many girls still hold on to the belief that falling in love and getting married is the ticket to lifelong happiness and financial security. Let your daughter know that for millions of women, this is a myth. Whether single by choice, divorced, or looking for a compatible mate, more and more women are single. (United States Census Bureau data reinforce the reality that more and more women are sole bread winners: between 1970 and 1996, the number of single women has doubled.)

In research by Girls Count (see page 167), 81 percent of teenage girls surveyed expected to be full-time moms, no longer working outside the home once they started a family. Belying the probability that this will occur is a 50 percent chance that first marriages occurring today will end in divorce.

Help your daughter understand that the future is unpredictable and girls must plan to be economically self-sufficient women. Single women may be the sole support of a household, and married women with children may need to work to help support the family.

Facts can help explode myths and misconceptions. Getting the facts on love, marriage, and money can encourage her to set goals and plan for the future. Finding out, for example, that the average income of divorced women who have custody of their children will be 21 percent lower than when they were married or that the more education a woman has, the more her salary approximates that of a man performing comparable work can influence your daughter's behavior.

Go on a fact hunt together. Visit the U.S. Census Bureau Web site (www.census.gov) and cruise the statistics. Want to know how many women are single? How many divorced? Divorced and raising kids? It's all there. Watch the newspaper for reports of government statistics and research by independent think tanks and foundations. Discuss how this information is related to this activity's topic and how it might affect a young woman's life-planning process.

No More Frogs to Kiss (page 147), which includes lots of interesting data about women and girls, is a gem of a book to help your daughter understand and face economic realities.

"That's one of my major things. I want to be totally self-reliant. You can't just depend on someone to take care of you."
—18-year-old editorial board member

"I think women should be as independent as possible. I think they should know how to manage and make their own money. That way they control their own lives."
—16-year-old survey respondent

91. Take Her to Work

Girls are interested in what their parents do all day. They want to meet their parents' co-workers and bosses and see the physical setting where they spend so much time. For mothers (and fathers) who work outside the home, this interest offers an opportunity to give girls a window on the world of work, as well as a chance to interact with a variety of adults.

Take Our Daughters to Work Day, sponsored by the Ms. Foundation, is probably the most well-known event designed to get girls into the workplace so they can learn firsthand about careers and work. Designed for girls age nine to fifteen, activities are organized around the country each spring on the last Thursday of April.

For more information about Take Our Daughters to Work Day, call the Ms. Foundation at 1-800-676-7780 or check out their web site at www.ms.foundation.org. (For more information about the event and a related book, *Girls Seen and Heard: 52 Lessons for Our Daughters*, see the "Career and Work" resource listings on page 160.)

Do take your daughter to work the last Thursday of each April, but don't stop there. If your employer allows kids to visit, arrange some times when your daughter can come in and work quietly on something while you go about your afternoon. If she's interested in a career or field someone else in your workplace is involved in, see if that person will let your daughter shadow her or him for an afternoon. If there are summer jobs in your company for teens, encourage her to apply.

"I've worked with my dad and it's really helped me understand the work ethic."
—17-year-old survey respondent

"Adults need to give girls as much information as they can about work, colleges, universities, self-empowerment conferences, and anything that could be useful for her while she's growing up."
—15-year-old survey respondent

92. Help Her Get an Inside View

A next step from taking your daughter to work is to help her get on the inside of work options she's interested in. Girls who get this inside view say it helps them decide more about what they want to pursue—and what they don't want to pursue. Opportunities to get an insider's perspective range from tours of work sites or spending a day shadowing someone to see what the job really involves and how people spend their day to finding a career mentor or working as an intern.

In an effort to educate kids about work, more and more schools are involved in coordinating tours, job shadowing, and internships. Check to see if these are available through your daughter's school. If not, work with her to find opportunities or, if options available through the school don't meet her needs, work with her to find an alternative. Encourage her to be assertive and proactive about hooking up with the right people or businesses by making phone calls, writing letters, or approaching someone after a talk.

One girl took on the task of finding an internship that would be meaningful to her by interviewing at businesses in her area of interest. She worked for extended periods of time at two graphic design firms. She ultimately got a job offer from one of the firms, but by then had seen enough to decide that the field was not for her!

> For more information about school-to-work opportunities and their benefits, contact the National School-to-Work Learning and Information Center, in the "Career and Work" resource listings, which start on page 160. One-on-one mentorships can also provide girls with role models and encouragement to pursue their interests. For help in finding a mentor for your daughter, contact the Mentoring Partnership at www.mentorship.org.

"I volunteered at the hospital and by working there I learned what it's like to be in a hospital environment because I want to be a doctor when I grow up."
    —16-year-old survey respondent

"One time for a school project, I had to write a letter to a person who had a career I might want. I wrote to a lawyer and she wrote back telling about being a lawyer and all the work it takes to get there. To this day, I occasionally take a look at the letter because it's an inspiration that all my hard work will one day pay off."
    —16-year-old survey respondent

"I want to become an FBI agent so I joined the Police Cadet Program at my local police department. I joined because I wanted to gain work experience in law enforcement. Being a cadet has taught me self-confidence and the ability to take charge and lead a group. The skills I have learned have helped me in my everyday life."
—17-year-old survey respondent

93. Open Options for Her

With an ever-expanding world of work options for women, help your daughter dream big and go after what she's really interested in. It might be something traditional, something you can relate to, or even something you secretly hoped she would be interested in. Or it might be something that surprises you, something you never imagined would interest her, like being an astronaut or a pilot. She might be interested in something nontraditional, like being a welder or mechanic. If she loves it, help her explore it.

Look into what educational requirements are involved. Find out typical salaries. Encourage your daughter to call people in the field to ask if she can do an informational interview, a twenty- or thirty-minute meeting in which she can ask about how to get into the field, what someone does all day, how she or he feels about it, and even talk about some aspects of the job that are not so great. Most people love to share their expertise. Many interviews last longer than twenty or thirty minutes, and some even lead to volunteer opportunities. Also encourage her to E-mail people with questions. It's a great way for busy professionals to share their expertise and provides another reason for your daughter to use the computer.

One way girls identify options is by taking career and preference tests in middle and high school. These experiences get mixed reviews. On the one hand, girls find them interesting. On the other, they feel pigeonholed, especially if the job or career seems far afield from anything a girl is interested in. One girl laughingly told of a career test that said she should be a mortician. Nothing could interest her less, and fortunately she's confident enough to ignore the results.

Certainly the results of these tests can be interesting and informative, and in many cases offer useful guidance. But in cases where the results are off base, girls should have the freedom to ignore them.

Give them that freedom and encourage them to participate in all kinds of activities that open a window on the diverse world of work.

Women and Work: In Their Own Words (see page 161) offers an inside view of women in diverse jobs and careers. If there is a community college in your area, contact them to see if they sponsor women's work and career fairs. Many do, and they're a great way to find out about options and learn about nontraditional careers for women. Also look for a copy of *Career Choices* (see page 160), which is designed specifically for teenage girls and young women.

"The summer before my junior year, I went to Space Camp/Aviation Challenge. Not only did I make lasting friendships, but I discovered my love of flying. As a result I started taking flying lessons and am now in AFROTC at college. I have never given up my dream of flying, but even if I don't become a pilot, I will still continue to do it as a hobby."
—18-year-old survey respondent

"Allow girls to break the mold and do things girls don't normally do. The saddest thing is to see a girl stifle herself from accomplishing her dreams because it is not ladylike."
—18-year-old survey respondent

94. Encourage an Entrepreneurial Bent

Not all girls are budding entrepreneurs, but for those who are, encourage it! Women's business ownership is a serious career option for young girls to consider. Growing by leaps and bounds in the last decades, one-third of all U.S. businesses are now owned by women, with those businesses employing more than 15 million workers in this country.

Business ownership can be an exciting choice for self-directed young women. It holds the promise of a career where they can do what they love, make a significant contribution, and have control over their destinies and financial futures.

Girls often get their first chance at serious money management by offering a service to neighbors. A step up from the lemonade stand, baby-sitting, dog-walking, and yard work are some of the kinds of things girls do to earn money. All these enterprises require important skills, from effective communication, scheduling, and decision-making to money management. And the skills translate directly to the larger workplace. Girls who have offered a neighborhood service say it helped boost their confidence when they went out looking for a "real" job in high school.

If your daughter has a plan for a business, ask her if she'd like to sit down and map out what she needs to do to get it off the ground. How will she publicize it? Will a flyer to neighbors do the job? Does she need money to get started? Offer to give her a business loan and work out a repayment schedule if she accepts. Will she need transportation or a special message on the answering machine?

Inspiring books for girls with an interest in owning a business include *No More Frogs to Kiss: 99 ways to Give Economic Power to Girls* and *Girls and Young Women Entrepreneurs: True Stories about Starting and Running a Business*, described in the "Business and Finance" resource listings on page 146. And don't neglect the other resources in this list, like Independent Means, which sponsors girls' business camps and competitions.

"I was on the original team of teen/women entrepreneurs in Girls Inc. that started a T-shirt design business from scratch. I realized anything is possible as long as you work hard toward it. I don't plan to be an entrepreneur as I get older, but it has helped me learn a lot of skills that will be useful in my life and that many women don't develop because they're told they can't, like budgeting, public speaking, and computer skills."

—19-year-old survey respondent

"I attended a wonderful all-girls camp called Camp $tart-Up and it was one of the best experiences of my life. I learned so much and was around such wonderful, powerful girls. It taught me that women can do anything."

—15-year-old survey respondent

95. Be a Money-Savvy Role Model

In almost 100 percent of the surveys in which girls said they felt pretty smart about money, they attributed much of their savvy to involvement of, and guidance by, parents who manage their money well and have financial goals themselves. In some cases, the parents were financial professionals of one sort or another or owned businesses or investment real estate. Daughters of accountants, real estate investors, financial officers, and business owners attributed their insight about or strategy for their financial futures to conversations and activities with their parents. One girl whose father is a finance director of a large organization credits him with helping her handle money issues appropriate for her age, from saving for a trip to Disneyland at ten and saving to buy a car at sixteen to starting an investment plan in college so she will have the down payment for a house when she graduates.

If you are not a financial or business professional, don't let that stop you. Let your daughter in on your financial life. Talk about how you manage your money, past financial goals and how you achieved them, and what some of your current financial goals are and how you're working to achieve those. When you're balancing your checkbook, show your daughter what you're doing. Let her make some of the calculations. Do you have a retirement plan at work or as part of a business you own? Talk about how much money you have in the account and how it will compound over time. Discuss penalties for early withdrawal so she understands how it encourages you to save. Do you have a household budget or general spending guidelines? Review them with her and talk about what you do when something comes up that stretches the budget. Get a copy

If money is not your friend and controls you more than you control it, try some self-help books like *Making the Most of Your Money* (Jane Bryant Quinn, Simon & Schuster) or *The Wall Street Journal Lifetime Guide to Money: Everything You Need to Know About Managing Your Finances—For Every Stage of Life* (C. Frederic Wiegold, Hyperion). Also visit www.independentmeans.com for good mother-daughter money-savvy ideas.

of your credit report and go over it with her. Discuss what it is and why it's important to have a good one.

Our culture has unflattering descriptions of money and wealth: filthy rich, dirt poor. Help your daughter develop a healthy attitude toward money and finances. Present her with a matter-of-fact approach that money and finances are necessities of life and encourage her to control them, rather than the other way around.

"I'm not an expert money manager, but I absolutely plan to manage my own money rather than having my husband do it for me. My parents divorced when I was young and I've grown up seeing my mother manage her own money. I never got the impression that this was not something women did. Now that I'm at college, I'm learning more about managing money. All my bills are sent to me, and even though my parents are paying for college, I'm learning to deal with things I never had to think about before. Lots of my friends just have all their bills sent directly to their parents."
—18-year-old advisory board member

"Helping my mom go grocery shopping taught me how to deal with money."
—18-year-old survey respondent

96. Talk About the Meaning of Money

As often as girls say they think money and money management are important, they also say money isn't everything. Part of a meaningful discussion about money needs to include ideas about its value.

When this topic comes up, girls talk about two aspects of the issue. First, that money is important but should not be an end in itself. And second, that it is dangerously easy in our materialistic society to let money rule you, rather than the other way around.

To help your daughter understand that money is a means, not an end, talk with her about its purpose. Jobs aren't great because they pay $50,000 a year; they're great because they're interesting and pay enough to support a healthy, secure lifestyle. Savvy girls are very aware of what people often give up in pursuit of money. They understand how people can be trapped by their need to support the "buying" habit and don't want to fall into that trap. Be a role model for your daughter by showing her simple pleasures, like hiking and spending time with good friends. Let her see there's more to life than shopping or the size of a bank account.

Girls describe a great antidote to letting money rule them: They calculate the number of hours they will have to work to buy something. When they see it will take four days to buy that new coat they love, last year's starts looking a lot better. If your daughter doesn't think in these terms, get her started. If she's earning her own money, walk through some examples with her. If you're the one who's buying, sit down with her and calculate how much of your time will be required to give her what she wants. Make a joint decision about whether to go ahead with the purchase.

In a society where advertising dangles the latest, greatest, unnecessary item before us twenty-four hours a day, where the bankruptcy rate has skyrocketed and support groups exist for people with buying habits they can't support, help your daughter avoid an out-of-control financial future by talking with her about the meaning of money.

> According to a report by the National Bankruptcy Review Commission, bankruptcy filings have increased sevenfold since the late 1970s.

"My father has always talked to me about the importance of saving, and having financial security. My parents always taught me that having money is having independence. They didn't talk about money as a value, but as security."
—17-year-old survey respondent

"Materialism is hard to overcome, but if I take a step back and look at what I've seen advertised it helps me understand why I want something. I feel a lot better about myself if I look into things, do some research, and look for a good deal or decide if I really need something."
—18-year-old editorial board member

"Although money is an important part of achieving success in our society, I feel too much emphasis is put on how much someone makes, rather than what they get out of the job."
    —18-year-old survey respondent

97. Track Spending

Some girls say parents require them to develop and maintain a budget. Others thought this was too strict, and even "anal," but all of the girls I've been in touch with agreed that having some way of keeping track of spending is important. As girls get older and are out and about more, they are surprised by how quickly money disappears. The fast-food snack, the bottle of juice, the first-run movies are all a serious drain on the pocketbook. When one girl realized the juice she was buying on her breaks at work was costing her $40 to $50 a month, she decided to mix up a big container at home so she could get the benefit of buying in bulk.

Tracking spending isn't a lifetime avocation. In most cases, a few weeks are eye-opening. If you've never done it, it can be an eye-opener for you too. Are you stopping at the espresso stand every day on your way to work? Have you ever calculated how that $75 or $100 a month could grow to pay for your daughter's college tuition if invested? Suggest to your daughter that you both keep an expenditures notebook for a week or two and compare notes. She—and you—will become aware of how "pocket" money is being spent, as well as larger expenditures. The experience usually has people saying they can't believe how much they've piddled away and motivates them to be more conscious of their spending. As girls pay for more and more of their own things, they also recognize the value of knowing where they're money is going. As one girl said, "When I was in middle school, twenty dollars seemed like a fortune. Now, it's gone in a day, especially if I don't pay attention to what I'm buying."

Girls who say they feel pretty good about their money management abilities have some kind of system for keeping track of where their money is going. It might be a definite budget or a less formal system in which girls have a good picture of what is due when. If car insurance needs to be paid every June and July, they save for that in between. If summer is coming and they want to have spending money for vacation, they fit in a little savings between buying things they need during the year. The idea is to help them become aware of where their money is going and how to have control over the spending process.

"I don't have a budget, but I know in my head what big expenses I have and I set a limit on my weekly spending depending on my expenses."
—18-year-old editorial board member

"I've always been careful with money because we don't have a great excess of it. One activity that helps me manage money is that every month before my mom gives me my allowance, she checks my budget book to make sure I've accounted for all the money I've spent."
—16-year-old survey respondent

"One activity that helped me manage my money was a summer Youth at Work program where I had to keep track of the money I made and how much I spent. I also set a goal of how much I would spend in a certain amount of time."
—18-year-old survey respondent

98. Show Her the Play Money

For many girls, it's a shock to find out what it takes to make it financially. Buying a car doesn't mean just saving up enough money to buy one; it means earning enough on an ongoing basis to pay for gas and insurance. Food, an apartment, entertainment, and other desires and needs add up fast. Help your daughter, especially as she gets into older adolescence, understand the number of dollars everyday life can eat up and the work required to earn them.

Girls who do appreciate what is involved in making it financially almost universally say they have had school or club role-playing experiences where they had to establish and follow a budget, invest in the stock market, find a job in the classified ads with a salary in their desired range, or in some other way pretend their way through real-life money experiences.

Try playing around with some money with your daughter. Research a company she thinks is cool, maybe a cosmetics company that has a no-animal-testing policy, and "invest" some money.

Check the stock on a daily or weekly basis and watch how it grows or shrinks. Make a month-by-month graph of your track record. Ask her to plan the budget for her dream party. Work out some scenarios together of how long it will take to save enough money for summer camp or a car if she puts aside different amounts for nine months.

Have some fun with it! Help her feel comfortable thinking about and managing money. Let her know money is a tool she can learn to use.

Lots of organizations offer fun "playing with money" experiences. Visit the JumpStart Coalition's Web site (www.jumpstartcoalition. org) where teens can take a fun on-line survey in the Mad Money Room to find out how their desired lifestyle lines up with their projected earning power. Girls Incorporated (see page 176) sponsors She's on the Money, an economic literacy program with lots of hands-on activities. Also take a look at programs offered by Junior Achievement and the National Council on Economic Education (in the "Business and Finance" resource listings on page 146) which include many simulated real-world money-management experiences.

"I think having economic control over your life is a key part in feeling good about yourself and your life. I remember this program I took called Money Works that helped me learn about managing money. For a week we were given a paycheck and we had to pay bills, buy groceries, all while working. It taught me a lot because it was fun in an educational way."
—16-year-old survey respondent

"It's unfortunate that in high school they give you the class Economics as a senior because I believe that's too late. People should be taught at an early age."
—19-year-old survey respondent

99. Bank on Her

Even the youngest pre-teen can benefit from starting a savings and checking account. With an account comes a monthly statement to

111

review with your daughter—even if the numbers haven't changed much from the previous one. Interest, bank charges, and fees for new checks also need to be considered. This early awareness helps girls understand that money comes from someplace. One girl laughed when she recounted how she would once tell her mother just to "write a check," when her mother was wishing for something she really couldn't afford. Now an older teen with a checking account of her own, she understands why her mother couldn't.

If she receives an allowance, encourage her to deposit any extra she has in one of her accounts. Explain that by putting money into her savings account she will actually be making money for herself through interest. Take a trip to the bank with her or coach her for a phone call when she's ready to move some of the savings account money to her checking account. With the first few checks she writes, show her how to deduct the amount from her balance, and when the first monthly statement comes, get out a calculator and reconcile her account together.

As your daughter gets older, her bank accounts and banking savvy offer a ready-made spot to help her pursue financial goals, whether to save for college, a car, a trip with her girls' club, or a new computer.

"I had a checking account from the time I was really little. My father had to co-sign with me, but now I really don't have any problem keeping money in my account and balancing it regularly."
—18-year-old editorial board member

"My parents guided me towards doing things correctly, like balancing my checking account, opening a savings account, paying bills and doing taxes, and I know I can take what I've learned and use it throughout my life."
—18-year-old survey respondent

100. Start an Investment Plan and Make Regular Contributions

It's surprising how many adults don't appreciate the value of time when working toward financial goals. Slow, steady investments coupled with the power of compounding add up. A hundred-dollar monthly investment made every month from the time a girl is fifteen until she is sixty-five will be worth a whopping $793,172 by the time she's sixty-five if invested at a modest 8 percent rate of return. At 10 percent, it will be worth $1,732,439. Not bad for an investment of only 60,000 real dollars!

By starting an investment plan for your daughter in a mutual fund or other investment tool when she is young, you can open many doors of opportunity: a college education, a down payment on a home, educational travel, or a secure retirement—not to mention an understanding and appreciation of how to make your money work for you, rather than always having to work for your money.

Encourage your daughter to invest by matching her dollar for dollar. Make a game of checking the balance on a regular basis and calculating the return. Review the statements together when they come, and brainstorm a list of good things to do with a percentage of the money that isn't earmarked for some specific thing, like college. Calculate what her balance will be worth in twenty years if she just lets it compound.

Foster an attitude in your daughter that she is in control of her financial future and help her get an early start toward accumulating the resources she'll need to reach her goals.

"My mother owns land and real estate and I learned from her. I now have investments in two mutual funds and if I am to accomplish my goals, I have to save and spend wisely. I also know I have to take risks on some investments."
—18-year-old survey respondent

"I have a friend whose parents started an investment account for her when she was really young to pay for college. Now she can use it, but only for going to school. I think that's really neat."
—18-year-old editorial board member

"I wasn't wise about money and therefore I never had any. One of my teachers gave me a challenge to focus on saving and that made me think about how I would do it. I was happy when I saw how much money I was saving. I saw things that I wanted, but I took on the challenge. I

became responsible with my money and many other things that crossed my path."

—17-year-old survey respondent

101. Give Her Some Credit

The spiraling bankruptcy rate shouldn't come as much of a surprise. Credit-card applications arrive in the mail almost daily. Buy now, pay-later plans entice the unwary, and advertisers spend millions to convince people they need the newest (often unnecessary) model or upgrade.

> The National Bankruptcy Review Commission attributes the increased bankruptcy rate, in part, to increasingly easy access to consumer credit.

One of the problems with credit, usually in the form of a credit card, is that it seems like magic: no money in the pocket, but you still get the goods. One girl described in dismay how a friend's use of her first credit card ended in disaster as she piled on new purchases, while never making more than the minimum payment.

If you're a money-savvy role model, show her the play money, track spending with her, talk about the meaning of money, and help her with bank accounts and investments, you'll help her get a head start on staying out of financial trouble. Understanding credit is another important building block in that head start.

Even the youngest teen can begin to buy responsibly on credit when you give her a loan for items that exceed her earnings or allowance. When there's something she's just got to have, work out a loan amount, repayment schedule, and interest rate. If she pays the loan off on time, take all the interest she's paid and add it to her investment or savings account. Reward her for being responsible. (If she pays the loan off early, consider a bonus contribution to her investment account.) If you're buying a house or other large-ticket item, like a new car, sit down with your daughter and calculate what the real cost is when interest is added in. For example, the real cost of a $15,000 car with a monthly payment of $359.19 at 7 percent interest over 48 months is approximately $17,240.00 when interest is added. Credit costs money. Cultivate a healthy respect for it by giving her some and showing her how it works.

"Working in a collection agency right out of high school has taught me so much about credit. I'm realizing it's a lot of work to keep up your credit. Girls need to understand what can happen if they're not careful."
—18-year-old editorial board member

"It's better to save a little off every paycheck or allowance for a rainy day. I wish I had learned to save when I was younger because nothing is better than to feel in control of your finances. You do not want credit companies calling you for bounced checks! So save when you can."
—20-year-old survey respondent

102. Help Her Earn It

By their own accounts, work is good for girls. Here are just a few of the benefits they say come from having to earn their own money and meet the requirements of a work commitment or job:

- An appreciation of the time required to earn money.
- An appreciation of the importance of managing and saving money.
- An understanding of how the world of work functions and what it takes to be successful in it.
- An increased awareness of the importance of education. (One girl said the best thing she ever did was take a dead-end job during the summer; no way was she going to end up without an education after high school.)

You can't beat that for one-stop shopping. What other single activity offers so many important benefits? You can get your daughter started on the "earn-it" mentality with jobs at home. Allowances can be earned or she can earn extra money by helping with household projects. Errands and jobs for neighbors can also be opportunities to earn, and to learn about following through on commitments to people outside the family. In addition, it begins to teach her how certain jobs are valued, based on the amount people will pay to have them done.

When she's old enough for "real" job opportunities, discuss what kinds of jobs she might find and how to incorporate one into her schedule so school doesn't get neglected. As she begins to earn money, discuss a money-management plan with her. If she has multiple goals, like saving for college, going to camp, and having pocket money, help her figure out how she needs to divide up her earnings. If she comes home with stories about personalities and problems at work, be a good listener and let her know that cultivating good work relationships takes effort.

Work will be a big part of your daughter's future. Set the stage for work opportunities and attitudes that will allow her to earn a good living, spend her days doing something she cares about, and continue growing and learning as an adult.

Girls' clubs like Girls Incorporated and the Girl Scouts (see "National Organizations" on page 174) offer many earning opportunities for girls that go far beyond the stereotype of selling cookies. These organizations offer your daughter opportunities to start businesses and work toward long-term financial goals, like members of my editorial board who worked for years to earn enough for their troop's Caribbean cruise.

"Having a job makes you appreciate the money you earn and makes you a little more careful about how you use it."
—Survey respondent (age not available)

"I've held several part-time jobs since the age of fifteen, including baby-sitting, house cleaning, service clerk, and produce clerk in a grocery store. Without joining the workforce during adolescence I would never have been able to experience some of the things I have. For example, I was able to earn money for my own car (my parents matched my funds). I've learned a lot about money by earning my own and learning how to handle it."
—18-year-old survey respondent

"I think if you want a lot of things, you should work to earn it. Then you have a feeling of satisfaction when you get it. I'm involved in a lot of expensive sports and I've had to work to buy the equipment. I think I appreciate and take better care of what I have than friends whose parents buy everything. It's okay sometimes to have someone support you financially, but you shouldn't become too dependent on it. You should always be ready to go out on your own."

—17-year-old survey respondent

Resource Listings

Quick-Find Guide

The following listings include all the publications, organizations, and materials mentioned in other parts of the book. Since many are referred to a number of times and don't necessarily relate to just one topic or chapter, the resources have been grouped in the categories below. This quick-find guide will help you locate the resources by topic. Many interesting things included in this chapter aren't mentioned in other parts of the book, so take some time to check them out, too. This chapter is intended to complement the resources referred to in the activity chapters.

These resources cover many different topics, but all have the common thread of helping girls make their voices heard by providing support for them to act and speak out on issues they care about. For more resources on activism related specifically to women's issues, check the "Gender Equity, Feminism, and Equal Rights" listings on page 163 and the list of girls' magazines (page 172), which also feature lots of information on activism.

Also look into programs offered through Girls Incorporated, the Girls Scouts, and other groups included in the "National Organizations" listings (page 174), many of which offer leadership training. The Web site Expect the Best from a Girl (www.academic.org) in the "Gender Equity, Feminism, and Equal Rights" resource listing also has information about leadership programs and camps for girls.

Books and Newsletters

Girls and Young Women Leading the Way: 20 True Stories about Leadership (Frances Karnes, Suzanne Bean, Free Spirit Publishing, 1993, 168 pp., $11.95).
Twenty-two activists who have made a difference in their communities tell their stories, offering girls inspiration and strategies they can use to act on issues they care about. A wide variety of activities is included, from recycling and feeding the hungry to promoting literacy. A how-to leadership section is included to give girls practical guidance in leadership and social action.

The Kid's Guide to Service Projects: Over 500 Service Ideas for Young People Who Want to Make a Difference (Barbara Lewis, Free Spirit, 1996, 184 pp., $10.95).
This step-by-step guide will help kids work for a cause they believe in, no matter how small or large. Potential causes, from the environment and animal rights to fighting hunger and crime, are described and instructions for creating petitions, flyers, and press releases and other support materials are included.

The Kid's Guide to Social Action: How to Solve the Social Problems You Choose—and Turn Creative Thinking Into Positive Action (Barbara Lewis, Free Spirit, 1998, 232 pp., $16.95).

This book is a must for any teen interested in working for a cause she believes in. Profiles of "kids in action" let girls see how much they really can do, and the how-to information guides them through the complete process from brainstorming and fund-raising to using the Internet to further their cause. Information about helpful organizations, Web sites, and books is included.

Things I Must Do Today

This great little newsletter bills itself as "news and tools for girls with better things to do than their hair," and delivers on that promise. Filled with information about organizations working for the environment, gender equity, and a host of other important issues, *Things I Must Do Today* offers personal action ideas (like how to make chemical-free sunscreen), and social and political action ideas (like how to write an effective letter or press release in support of a cause you care about). The publisher also offers a line of action kits called Real Girls' Guides to Life to help girls make a difference, featuring activities from setting up a school recycling program or planning a boycott to starting a small business.

For more information, contact:
Things I Must Do Today
P.O. Box 13947
Berkeley, CA 94712

ORGANIZATIONS AND WEB SITES

InterAction Website

A coalition of 150 organizations, this site provides interesting reading material about social action work in the United States and other countries around the world, including gender-equity issues. Suggestions for activities and links to other related sites are included. Visit the site at www.interaction.org.

Kids for a Cleaner Environment

To get a flavor of just how much a girl can do who has her mind set on making a difference, check out what Melissa Poe has accomplished. At nine, she founded Kids for a Cleaner Environment and built the volunteer organization into an international 300,000-member organization. (When Melissa turned eighteen, she stepped down as president and turned the reins over to two younger girls.)

The organization's newsletter, *Kids F.A.C.E.*, is read by more than 3 million people around the globe.

For more information, contact:
Kids for a Cleaner Environment
P.O. Box 158254
Nashville, TN 37215
(615) 331-77381
www.kidsface.org

National Indian Youth Leadership Project (NIYLP)

This organization sponsors local and national programs for Native American youth, emphasizing service to their communities and peers. NIYLP hosts a leadership camp for young people and a sports program, and provides training for teachers interested in incorporating service learning into their curricula. Drug- and abuse-prevention programs that address the special needs of the Native American population are also offered.

For more information, contact:
National Indian Youth Leadership Project
P.O. Box 2140
Gallup, NM 87305
(505) 722-9176
www.cia-g.com/~niylp

The National Youth in Action Campaign

This campaign is designed to provide an avenue for teens and young adults to have greater involvement in, and influence over, important issues affecting their lives. As a part of the campaign, a *Youth Action Guide* was developed to help teens design local and national programs to encourage diversity and inclusiveness, improve the environment, create greater access to health care and prevention information, fight against violence and hate crimes, and improve human suffering through human-rights work. Action Award Grants of up to $1,000 for well-designed programs are available. The campaign sponsors an annual youth convention and collaborates with a wide range of educational, social, and cultural organizations. Teens can log on to the Web site and voice their opinions in an on-line game called Change the World: A Game We All Can Win.

For more information, contact:
National Youth in Action Campaign
Foundation of America
43 Malaga Cove Plaza
Suite D
Palos Verdes Estates, CA 90274
(619) 576-4044
www.youthlink.org

National Youth Advocacy Coalition (NYAC)

The coalition is a national organization whose sole mission is to advocate for and address issues affecting gay and lesbian, bisexual, and transgender youth by offering training for, and keeping communication open between, community-based and national organizations, as well as working to influence public policy. Support for youth organizing and activism is provided. NYAC's Bridges Project publishes resource information, including the magazine *Crossroads* and a series of information packets on education, religion, gender identity, and other topics that affect young people in this population.

For more information, contact:
National Youth Advocacy Coalition
1711 Connecticut Ave. NW
Suite 206
Washington, DC 20009
(202) 319-7596
www.nyacyouth.org

!OutProud!

!OutProud!, the National Coalition for Gay, Lesbian, Bisexual, and Transgender Youth, provides resources for youth and educators about sexual orientation, including a School Resources Library and information about other national, regional, and local organizations that teens can contact for support and information. The organization's Web site offers on-line brochures about sexual orientation, a search engine to identify useful books, a message board, a clickable map to find local organizations, and links to other sites. !OutProud! also publishes a booklet of state-by-state organizations young people can turn to for help.

For more information, contact:
!OutProud!
369 Third St.
Suite B-362
San Rafael, CA 94901
(415) 460-5452
www.outproud.org

Parents, Families and Friends of Lesbians and Gays
If your daughter is gay or has friends who are gay and you are struggling to understand, or you want to provide support or receive support yourself, this organization can help. For gay youth (and their straight friends), sexual orientation can become an avenue for activism and self-expression. Parental and adult understanding and support can be an important part of self-acceptance and constructive action.

For more information, contact:
Parents, Families and Friends of Lesbians and Gays
1101 14th St., NW
Suite 1030
Washington, DC 20005
(202) 638-4200
www.pflag.org

Third Wave Direct Action Corp.
Third Wave is a nonprofit activist organization for young feminists working for social change. Based in New York, it has affiliates in Minneapolis/St. Paul and San Francisco. Their quarterly newsletter is full of facts to stimulate girls to action, information about organizations to support, and articles on critical issues like reproductive rights and equal pay for equal work. The Third Wave Fund, designed to support women's and feminist issues, has a Micro-Enterprise Fund for Young Women, a National Fund for Reproductive Rights, the Digikids Fund (to encourage computer skills in girls), and other grants. (For information about other organizations working for gender equity, review the "Gender Equity, Feminism, and Equal Rights" resource listing on page 163.) Joining buys a subscription to the quarterly newsletter.

For more information, contact:
Third Wave Direct Action Corp.
116 East 16th St., 7th Floor
New York, NY 10003
(212) 388-1898

Who Cares Magazine

Started by two young activist women, *Who Cares* describes itself as a tool kit for social change. It's a free full-color magazine, published six times a year, designed to offer guidance for people working to improve social and environmental conditions through nonprofit and entrepreneurial ventures. Leaders in the field are profiled and concrete strategies for action and change are covered.

For more information and to receive a sample magazine, contact:
Who Cares Magazine
1511 K St. NW, Suite 412
Washington, DC 20005
(202) 628-1691
www.whocares.org

The Young Women's Leadership Initiative

Sponsored by the Center for the American Woman and Politics, a research, education, and public service center focusing on women's participation in and contributions to American politics, the Young Women's Leadership Initiative is a training program that includes a summer institute and a year-long follow-up leadership project. (Even if your daughter is not interested in the leadership program, visit the center's Web site, where you can learn about women politicians and review voting-related issues, like sex differences in voter turnout.)

For more information, contact:
Center for the American Woman and Politics
Eagleton Institute of Politics
Rutgers University
New Brunswick, NJ 08901
(732) 932-9384
www.rci.rutgers.edu/~cawp/

The books in this list are in alphabetical order. This is a general list of good books for girls. For information about more good books on specific topics, like sports or science, check the appropriate resource listings.

33 Things Every Girl Should Know: Stories, Poems and Smart Talk by 33 Extraordinary Women (Tonya Bolden, editor, Crown Publishing, 1998, 160 pp., $13.00).

Thirty-three hot women of our times, from Rebecca Lobo and Natalie Merchant to Alice Hoffman and Sigourney Weaver, reflect on their teen and growing-up years with humor, insight, and the perspective of a successful passage. Girls will be inspired, motivated, and consoled by this collection of very personal writings by a diverse group of interesting, accomplished women. Authors, artists, scientists, scholars, entrepreneurs, athletes, and others are included, letting girls know there is a world of possibility open to them.

Any Girl Can Rule the World (Susan Brooks, Fairview Press., 1998, 224 pp., $12.95).

This is a fun, hip book that encourages girls to get out there and do it! Whatever it is they want to do, they'll probably find help in this book of ideas and resources. From starting your own business or investing in the stock market to working for your favorite cause or learning about a cool career through an internship, *Any Girl Can Rule the World* offers inspiration, ideas, contacts, and action plans.

Brave New Girls: Creative Ideas to Help Girls Be Confident, Healthy and Happy (Jeanette Gadeberg and Beth Hatlen, Fairview Publishing, 1997, 192 pp., $12.95).

A combination workbook, personal journal, and idea book, *Brave New Girls* covers all the topics teenage girls grapple with, and helps them sort throught their feelings and experiences. Money management, family, school, body image, and other topics on girls' minds are covered. True stories from teenage girls about their successes are included. A good book for mothers and daughters to use together.

Choices: A Young Woman's Guide to Self-Awareness and Personal Planning (Mindy Bingham and Sandy Stryker, Academic Innovations, 1993, 240 pp., $19.95).
The workbook-style approach of this book offers girls a hands-on, fact-filled guide to understanding issues involved in planning their futures. Filled with quizzes, research suggestions, and personal-exploration exercises, it covers careers, salaries, nontraditional work options, budgeting, goal-setting, assertiveness, and a host of other topics necessary for life planning. Real girls' stories are included and lend impact to the importance of the topics covered. (The publisher has a variety of related materials and books. They can be contacted at www.academicinnovations.com or at 805-967-8015).

Finding Our Ways: The Teen Girls' Survival Guide (Allison Abner and Linda Villarosa, HarperPerennial, 1996, 336 pp., $13.00).
Based on interviews with teen girls from a variety of backgrounds, this guide offers girls a multicultural perspective on growing up. Discussions cover everything from common topics like body image, relationships, and sexual development to less frequently discussed topics like body piercing and plastic surgery. The book emphasizes the importance of girls' involvement in the community around them, and provides information about how to become involved in issues they care about.

For Girls Only: Wise Words, Good Advice (Carol Weston, Avon Camelot, 1998, 195 pp., $5.99).
Popular girls' advice columnist Carol Weston brings together hundreds of quotes to guide and inspire girls in friendship, school, family life, love, work, and other areas of their lives. From Maya Angelou and Oprah Winfrey to Socrates and Ralph Waldo Emerson, authors, philosophers, poets, artists, and other groundbreakers—past and present—are included.

Girl Power: Young Women Speak Out (Hillary Carlip, Warner Books, 1995, 335 pp., $13.99).
Girls between the ages of thirteen and nineteen write about their fears, dreams, and hopes, helping other girls understand themselves. Writers come from a variety of backgrounds (teen mothers, gang members, sorority girls), offering diverse perspectives and provoking

insights about growing up as a girl in our society. The author also has a Web site (www.girlpower.com) where girls can post their own ideas and read what other girls have to say.

Girls: An Anthology (Edith Chevat, Laurie Piette, and Angie Argabrite, eds., Global City Press, 1997, 367 pp., $14).
This collection of stories, poems, interviews, essays, and letters written by girls and women ages fourteen to eighty offers girls an inside look at what it means to be a girl growing up in America. Writings by women like author Maya Angelou, sculptor Fay Chaing, and others let girls know they are not alone with their own fears, experiences, confusion, and hopes.

Girl Talk: Staying Strong, Feeling Good, Sticking Together (Judith Harlan, Walker & Co., 1997, 128 pp., $8.95).
A playful, encouraging look at ways girls can hang on to their active pre-adolescent selves during the teenage years. Filled with activity ideas and inspiring facts about women who have made a difference, this book offers girls things they can do every day to maintain their confidence and self-esteem.

The Girls' Guide to Life: How to Take Charge of the Issues That Affect You (Catherine Dee, Little Brown, 1997, 147 pp., $14.95).
A fun activity guide for girls, this book provides lots of ideas and information to get them thinking about how they're treated by others, how they treat themselves, and how society treats women in general. Covers a wide range of topics like self-esteem, media coverage of women and girls, sexual harassment, career and work, the arts, and much more. Includes inspiring quotes from successful women, interesting facts and data from gender research, and profiles of successful young women.

Girls Know Best: Advice for Girls from Girls on Just About Everything (Edited by Michelle Roehm, Beyond Words Publishing, 160 pp., 1997, $8.95).
This collection of essays by girls six to sixteen covers light-hearted, humorous, and serious topics that all girls will relate to. A combination of advice and storytelling about girls' own experiences, here girls can find out what other thoughtful, articulate girls are thinking

and feeling about topics as diverse as teen depression, racial differences, and how to avoid life's most embarrassing moments. Photos, illustrations, and an introduction by gold-medal Olympic gymnast Kerri Strug add to the impact. (Teen writers can enter a contest to have their work considered for publication in this annually released book. Get contest details and entry information from the Girls Know Best writers' contest described on page 180.)

Girls Know Best 2: Tips on Life and Fun Stuff to Do (Edited by Michelle Roehm, Beyond Words Publishing, 1998, 120 pp., $8.95). More of the same kind of great stuff found in the book described above.

Girls Speak Out: Finding Your True Self (Andrea Johnston, foreword by Gloria Steinem, Scholastic, 128 pp., 1997, $17.95).
Based on Girls Speak Out workshops the author conducted across the country with girls ages nine to fifteen, this book offers strategies for building self-esteem and self-acceptance. Readers get a window into the workshops where women and girls met to share their hopes, dreams, and fears and to learn about the importance of listening to their "true selves." Stories, poems, and discussions let girls know they are not alone, and stimulate them to get to know, and accept, who they really are.

Girl Talk: All the Stuff Your Sister Never Told You (Carol Weston, HarperPerennial, 1997, 352 pp., $14.00).
This book by the popular girls' advice columnist gets rave reviews from girls, who say, "It's like the big sister I never had." It covers important topics for girls from money, drugs, education, sex, friends, and family in an upbeat practical way. One hundred and sixty letters from teens are included.

Growing Up Feeling Good (Ellen Rosenberg, Puffin, 1996, 512 pp., $13.99).
While not written just for girls, this is a great reference book for young people. It's broken into two major sections, "Growing Up Feeling Good About Your Body" and "Growing Up Feeling Good About Yourself," where teens can find information and guidance on any topic imaginable from AIDS, breast development, eating dis-

orders, friendship, and sibling rivalry to stepfamilies. The information is easy to find and is chunked up into manageable sizes with good descriptive headings that make it easy to identify where to go for help on a specific topic.

The Me Nobody Knew: A Story of Triumph for All Girls (Shannon McLinden, Lerner Publications, 1998, 112 pp., $5.98).
A true story written by a girl who struggled with, and overcame, self-destructive behaviors and the pain of sexual abuse. The author struggled with a drinking problem, hated her looks, starved herself, and always felt unpopular. Her story and efforts to heal will help girls everywhere who struggle with feelings of inadequacy and low self-esteem.

My Feelings, My Self (Lynda Madaras with Area Madaras, Newmarket Press, 1993, 160 pp., $9.95).
By the authors of the bestselling *My Body, My Self: The What's Happening to My Body? Workbook for Girls*, this bestselling workbook-style guide is filled with great information, exercises, and activities to help your daughter navigate adolescence thoughtfully. Chapters on friends, parents, peer pressure, relationships, popularity, and "best friends" will give her concrete ways to handle difficult situations. A section on problem-solving and effective communication in the "Parents" chapters are useful for school and social relationships as well as for communicating with family members.

Real Girl Real World: Tools for Finding Your True Self (Heather Gray and Samantha Phillips, Seal Press, 1998, pp., 221, $14.95).
Honest, straightforward discussions on a wide range of topics offer insight and facts that will help girls take charge of their lives. A chapter on feminism provides a context for the take-charge approach encouraged throughout the book. Eating disorders, media influence on body image, sexual assault, being in love and in charge, and other similar issues are covered. Sidebars with supporting facts and stories from girls add power and interest.

Sugar in the Raw: Voices of Young Black Girls in America (Rebecca Carroll, Crown, 1997, 144 pp., $12.00).

In this compilation of girls' stories, based on interviews and first-person narratives, readers get a picture of what it means to grow up black and female today. Girls ages eleven to twenty from urban and rural areas all across the country speak eloquently and passionately about the confusion and contradictions they confront in their daily lives. Unfiltered stories about teachers who assumed black girls wouldn't know the answer, girls who transferred out of classes because they were harassed by white girls, a lesbian who grapples with being black and gay, and others will help girls of every color understand what it means to be a black girl in America.

The Teen Trip (Gayle Kimball, Equality Press, 1997, 523 pp., $16.95). This book revolves around quotes by over 1,500 young people who talk about what's on their minds and how they deal with difficult issues. Chapters, each including quotes, information, and resources, cover topics like peers, family, school, community involvement, drugs, sexuality, and others. Information specifically for girls is included. In addition to providing information on important topics, this is a good book for girls to read to learn about how other girls and boys feel about important issues. You can also visit the author's Web site (www.ecst.csuchico.edu/~gkimball), which has links to other sites of interest, including a list of feminist electronic newsletters.

BOOKS ABOUT GOOD BOOKS FOR GIRLS

One of the most effective ways to influence how girls think about girls' and women's roles and possibilities in the world is to surround them with role models—real and imagined. The books in this list will help you select fiction and nonfiction reading for your daughter that fits her interests and reading level.

100 Books for Girls to Grow On (Shireen Dodson, HarperCollins, 1998, 334 pp., $14.00).
By the author of *The Mother-Daughter Book Club* (see page 132), this book is a feast of reading-related ideas and activities for mothers and daughters who want to share the reading experience. Each of the descriptions includes activity ideas for related crafts, cooking, movies, and field trips to help the reading come alive and strengthen the mother-daughter relationship.

500 Great Books by Women: A Reader's Guide (Erica Bauermeister, Jesse Larsen, Holly Smith, Penguin USA, 1994, 425 pp., $12.95).
For parents looking for books by and about women to share with their older daughters, this guide provides a well-annotated reading list. Books are organized by theme and cross-referenced by date, country, historical period, and other categories for easy selection of books based on specific interests. The book itself makes great reading and provides clear evidence of women's literary accomplishments.

Brave Girls and Strong Women Booklist.
Compiled by a teenage girl, this list includes books from small presses that provide strong, brave female role models. The books are divided into three categories (Young Readers: ages 2–7; Middle Readers: ages 7–14; and Older Readers: ages 12 and up), so it's easy to find age-appropriate titles. Fiction, self-help, history, and biographies are included. You can check out the list at http://members.aol.com/brvgirls or send $1.00 to Jyotsna Sreenivasan at P.O. Box 15481, Washington, D.C. 20003-0481, for a printed list.

Great Books for Girls: More Than 600 Books to Inspire Today's Girls and Tomorrow's Women (Kathleen Odean, Ballantine, 1997, 420 pp., $12.95).
This bibliography features books with strong female protagonists who are not waiting around to participate in someone else's action. They are strong, resourceful women and girls with their own dreams and ambitions. Descriptions are divided into chapters by type (biographies, novels, mysteries, etc.) and age-appropriateness, so it's easy to select titles for pre-teens and teenagers. (Books have been selected for readers from age six to fourteen, but many older girls will enjoy the books selected for young teenagers.) Succinct, well-written descriptions of each book provide good information for book selection.

Let's Hear It for Girls: 375 Great Books for Readers 2 to 14 (Erica Bauermeister, Holly Smith, Penguin USA, 1997, 240 pp., $10.95).
Organized by reading level, this book makes it easy for parents to identify books with strong, resourceful female protagonists appro-

priate for the pre-teen and early teenage girl. Whether you're looking for fictional or real role models, *Let's Hear It for Girls* will steer you to books that feature inspiring women and girls from around the world, and from different historical periods.

The Mother-Daughter Book Club: How Ten Busy Mothers and Daughters Came Together to Talk, Laugh, and Learn Through Their Love of Reading (Shireen Dodson, HarperCollins, 1997, 296 pp., $12.95).
This book is both an inspiration and a guide for mothers who want to open the channels of communication with their daughters by reading together. In this account of the author's experience starting her book club, she includes practical how-to information for starting your own. Reading lists and participant comments are included.

The Movie Mom
Watching movies together can be a great way to stimulate discussions with your daughter. Nell Minow will help you pick movies that are appropriate for your daughter's age and issues she may be grappling with, or steer you to movies about strong women who have affected their world and the people around them. Visit her Web site at www.moviemom.com for guidance, where you'll find tips and guidelines for selecting movies, reviews of current video and theater releases, and ways to get your kids involved in watching good movies that are off the beaten blockbuster track. Also look for her book (*The Movie Mom's Guide to Family Movies*, Avon), which includes a chapter on selecting movies with strong female role models.

BOOKS AND NEWSLETTERS FOR ADULTS

These books and newsletters are listed in alphabetical order. While you're looking for a specific book mentioned in an activity chapter, take the time to find out about the other books in this list since many are not referred to in other parts of the book. Also check the other resource listings for books on specific topics (e.g., eating disorders in "Body Image and Media Representation of Women").

BOOKS

All That She Can Be: Helping Your Daughter Maintain Her Self-Esteem (Carol Eagle, Fireside, 1994, 252 pp., $11.00).
A practical look at how to prevent the drop in self-esteem girls experience as they enter adolescence. Body image, sexuality, dating, academics, peer pressure and friendship, and other issues related to intellectual, emotional, and social development are covered. The author offers specific phrases to use in tricky situations to help parents ease into difficult conversations. Especially useful are the guide for evaluating whether your daughter is at risk and the discussion of how your own unresolved childhood issues may affect your daughter.

Celebrating Girls: Nurturing and Empowering Our Daughters (Virginia Beame Rutter, Conari Press, 1996, 195 pp., $10.95).
This book offers ways to celebrate girls and help them feel good about being female in the seemingly mundane activities of daily life, like hair brushing, and in the more special events, like the start of menstruation. Common girls' activities, like body adornment and artistic expression, are respected and looked at from the perspective of how they help girls understand themselves and their world. Lots of practical activity suggestions are included.

Cherishing Our Daughters: How Parents Can Raise Girls to Become Confident Women (Evelyn Bassoff, Putnam, 1999, 288 pp., $13.95).
This mother and psychologist offers advice and practical ideas for parents who want to raise self-confident, successful girls. Covering all aspects of development, Bassoff helps parents understand how to deal with complex issues like sexual development, rebellion, overcoming disappointment, and providing security without being overprotective. She also addresses body-image issues, offering specific ways to help girls tie their feelings of self-worth to what they do, not how they look. Her approach is compassionate and directed toward all parents, including mothers, fathers, single parents, adoptive parents, and gay and lesbian parents.

The Difference: Discovering the Hidden Ways We Silence Girls (Judith Mann, Warner Books, 1996, 317 pp., $11.99).

Based on her own desire to understand the frequent emotional derailment girls experience as they enter adolescence—and to prevent it in her own daughter—journalist Judith Mann interviewed psychologists, educators, parents, and teenage girls in an effort to understand why so many girls become silenced during adolescence. Integrated with these interviews is an investigation of the historical, sociological, religious, and political roots of a society that accepts the frequent humiliation and degradation of women and girls. The result is a heartfelt call for change in the ways we raise boys and girls, with constructive suggestions for how this can be accomplished.

Don't Stop Loving Me: A Reassuring Guide for Mothers of Adolescent Daughters (Ann Caron, Henry Holt, 1991, 228 pp., $13.00).
This book guides parents through the stages of a girl's adolescence with down-to-earth information about what girls are experiencing during the teenage years. Sex, peer pressure, discipline, physical changes, and family relationships, including a daughter's evolving relationship with her father, are covered. Particularly valuable is a discussion of how the mother-daughter relationship changes during adolescence and how to build a relationship that will last into adulthood.

For All Our Daughters: How Mentoring Helps Girls and Young Women Master the Art of Growing Up (Pegine Echevarria, Chandler House, 1998, 228 pp., $14.95).
The author makes a heartfelt and compelling case for getting adult women involved in the lives of girls and young women, describing how mentors and mentoring can help girls develop in key areas of their lives (physical, intellectual, emotional, spiritual, and financial accountability) and act as role models for handling life's challenges. She makes important distinctions between a parent's and a mentor's role, stressing that both are needed for girls to experience the full range of possibilities open to them as they grow up. Parents looking for guidance in how to select and evaluate a mentor and women interested in becoming mentors will find the information they need, along with a good dose of inspiration.

Fathering: Strengthening Connection with Your Children No

Matter Where You Are (Will Glennon, Conari Press, 1995, 219 pp., $10.95).

Fathering uses vignettes from many fathers' lives to reveal the issues men face when they become parents—a role many men feel ill equipped to take on. Discussing the difficulty men often have in expressing their emotions and the differences in how men and women are accepted and supported in the parental role, this book helps men understand how they can be loving, responsible parents and establish respectful, honest relationships with their children.

Growing a Girl (Barbara Mackoff, Dell, 1996, 275 pp., $12.95).

Emphasizing how to help girls become strong, active, and confident from birth, this book is intended as preventative medicine for parents who want to help their daughters avoid the common drop in self-esteem girls experience around puberty. Lots of practical ideas for avoiding sex-stereotyping, building interest in math, science, and team sports, and generally fostering self-reliance are included. Statistics and research findings reinforce the ideas presented, and personal anecdotes make the issues real.

How to Father a Successful Daughter (Nicky Marone, Fawcett, 1998, 317 pp., $12.95).

This book looks at the special relationship between daughters and fathers, providing specific suggestions to promote girls' self-respect and confidence. Fathers are encouraged to avoid being overprotective and will learn how to encourage their daughters to be bold, take reasonable risks, and set goals. Ways fathers' attitudes and comments can affect their daughters' body images are also covered, with concrete ideas for helping girls avoid eating disorders and an obsession with weight.

How to Mother a Successful Daughter: A Practical Guide to Empowering Girls from Birth to Eighteen (Nicky Marone, Harmony Books, 1998, 304 pp., $25.00).

This is a down-to-earth guide for mothers who want to help their daughters overcome cultural stereotypes that often affect their self-esteem and confidence. The author starts from the premise that mothers can be positive role models and offers lots of fun, practical ways to influence girls, from learning new skills with them to cultivating an interest in math, science, sports, and other activities that are known to build girls' self-esteem.

How to Talk So Kids Will Listen and Listen So Kids Will Talk
(Adele Faber, Elaine Mazlish, Avon, 1991, 242 pp., $12.00).
This book, first released in 1982, has stood the test of time for good reason. It offers down-to-earth advice about how to keep the channels of communication open between you and your children. Step-by-step exercises, reminder pages, and cartoons illustrating the points make it a practical and very usable book. Respect, problem-solving, and consistency are stressed.

Mother-Daughter Choices: A Handbook for the Coordinator
(Mindy Bingham, Judith Edmondson, and Sandy Stryker, Academic Innovations, 1997, 192 pp., $14.95).
A guidebook for setting up and running a mother-daughter group to explore what it means to be a woman in today's society. Career exploration, work, money management, relationships, health, and other topics are covered, while practical exercises, like setting up a household budget and exploring work options to support the budget, are included on each topic. This program is used by groups around the country, including Girls Incorporated (see page 176). The publisher has a variety of related materials and workbooks. Contact them at www.academicinnovations.com or at (805) 967-8015.

Mother-Daughter Revolution: From Good Girls to Great Women
(Elizabeth Debold, Marie Wilson, and Idelissi Malave, Bantam, 1994, 371 pp., $11.95).
This book offers mothers a way to help daughters remain true to themselves and resist the common practice of cutting themselves off from their true feelings and desires. Beginning with a thoughtful analysis of how and why this occurs, the authors move to what they call three resistance strategies: reclaiming (mothers reclaiming their own lost adolescent selves), voice lessons (learning to "listen" to yourself and your daughter, and give voice to honest feelings), and joining (working with girls to provide the information and knowledge needed to resist limiting concepts about girls and women).

Positive Parenting for Teens: The A to Z Book of Sound Advice and Practical Solutions (Karen Renshaw Joslin and Mary Bunting Decher, Free Spirit, 1994, 432 pp., $12.95).
This is an eminently practical book for busy parents who want to do the right thing. Each entry includes information about how to prevent problems, offers sample dialogues for talking through an issue, and provides guidance in when and how to seek outside help. Covers every relevant topic imaginable in an easy-to-find format.

Raising Strong Daughters (Jeanette Gadeberg, Fairview Press, 1996, 264 pp., $12.95).
A guide to helping your daughter gain the confidence and strength she'll need for a successful adulthood, this book encourages parents to help girls be uppity, in the best sense of the word: voicing their opinion, knowing what they want—and don't want, thinking about and planning for the future, being physically strong, and other attributes that will help them control their own destinies. Parents will find a wealth of fun, practical suggestions for things to do for and with their daughters.

Reviving Ophelia: Saving the Selves of Adolescent Girls (Mary Pipher, Ballantine, 1995, 304 pp., $12.95).
This book of case studies and analysis thrust into the public eye the challenges girls face in trying to grow up healthy and happy in our complex, media-dominated culture. Pipher discusses girls' loss of confidence, decreased involvement in pre-adolescent activities, and unhealthy obsession with body image and weight as a loss of self in a society she describes as "girl poisoning." A must-read for parents who want to understand what girls face as they leave the pre-teen years, the book is filled with concrete suggestions for helping girls retain their pre-adolescent confidence and zest for life.

The Roller Coaster Years: Raising Your Child Through the Maddening Yet Magical Middle School Years (Charleen Gianneti and Margaret Sagarese, Broadway Books, 1997, 308 pp., $25.00).
This book offers parents help with the in-between stage when their daughters aren't kids anymore, but they're not quite teens either. Filled with specific suggestions, things to say, and new ways to think about your child's behavior, the book is designed to build

and maintain connections and constructive influence with your daughter during a period when she is seeking more independence. All areas of development (intellectual, emotional, and physical) are covered, along with special topics like drugs, harassment, and sexuality.

The Shelter of Each Other: Rebuilding Our Families (Mary Pipher, Grosset/Putnam, 1997, 282 pp., $12.95).
The author of the groundbreaking book *Reviving Ophelia* offers a vision of how life can work for families by building cooperative, interconnected families and communities. Strongly critical of our plugged-in, overloaded consumer lifestyle, Pipher offers suggestions for rituals and activities to counteract these trends and establish a meaningful lifestyle of contribution and connection. Compelling examples and case studies of people who have made the change are included.

Things Will Be Different for My Daughter: A Practical Guide to Building Her Self-Esteem and Self-Reliance (Mindy Bingham and Sandy Stryker, Penguin Books, 1995, 494 pp., $14.95).
This book helps parents go beyond some of the disappointments of child-rearing in a post-feminist era that still sees girls longing to look like Barbie and hoping for Prince Charming to arrive on a white horse. Using a workbook approach with lots of practical ideas, this book covers development from birth through the teen years. Its breadth and density make it best used as a topic-by-topic guide to be drawn on when specific issues arise, like dating, homework, and sports participation. The book covers all the important topics, such as math and science participation, the importance of physical activity in building self-esteem, success in school, finding a special talent, and more. Also included is an "emancipation schedule" of tasks, like performing breast exams and money-management activities, to build your daughter's self-reliance and confidence.

NEWSLETTERS

New Moon Network: For Adults Who Care About Girls
Published by the people who founded *New Moon: The Magazine for Girls and Their Dreams*, this newsletter gives voice to the ideas of parents and other adults who care about and work with girls. The variety of articles and the thoughtful, practical ideas discussed make

this a great publication for parents who face the myriad feelings and events that swirl in a growing girl's universe. From a father who reports on his involvement with his daughter's soccer team to a psychologist with practical suggestions for discussing divorce to an interview with the author of the *American Girl* book series, plus quick takes on books, videos, and other resources, New Moon Network is a gold mine in every issue.

For more information, contact:

New Moon Network
P.O. Box 3587
Duluth, MN 55803
(800) 381-4743
www.newmoon.org

Daughters: A Newsletter for Girls Age Eight to Eighteen

If you're looking for a source of information from experts in every field imaginable that affects girls' lives, this is the newsletter to subscribe to. Every issue includes several feature stories complemented by lots of brief articles and book reviews. Feature articles and briefs offer practical ideas for dealing with difficult issues (like what to say and how to respond if your daughter has been drinking), as well as background information to help you think about how to maintain a close, constructive relationship with your daughter as she grows and changes.

For more information, contact:

Daughters
1808 Ashwood Ave.
Nashville, TN 37212
(800) 829-1088
www.daughtersnewsletter.com

BODY IMAGE AND MEDIA REPRESENTATION OF WOMEN

This listing focuses on topics that affect how girls feel about their bodies and topics that relate to those feelings, like eating disorders. For more information about sexuality and helping your daughter make smart decisions in this arena, look over the "Staying Safe and in Control" resource listings on page 88 and pay close attention to organizations like Advocates for Youth and Sexuality Information and Education Council of the U.S. (SIECUS).

BOOKS AND MAGAZINES

The Body Project (Joan Jacobs Brumberg, Random House, 1997, 267 pp., $24.00).

In this fascinating comparison of girls' adolescence now and in Victorian times, Brumberg reveals a shift in how young women derive a sense of self-worth. Using diary entries of young women in the nineteenth and early twentieth centuries and today, she shows that self-worth used to be based in large part on contributions to the family, and on service to the community and God. More recent entries reflect a preoccupation with weight and appearance and feelings of inadequacy as young women compare themselves to images of women they see in advertising. This book encourages women to become involved in and protective of girls as they go from pre-adolescence to early womanhood, and offers a thought-provoking basis for conversation with girls, who often believe that advertised images are the best and only way to look.

Full and Fulfilled: The Science of Eating to Your Soul's Satisfaction (Nan Allison and Carol Beck, AB Books, 1998, 172 pp, $12.95).

For parents who have unresolved eating and body image issues that will undoubtedly affect their daughter, this book offers practical ways to have a healthier relationship with food and eating. Based on the concept of "intuitive" eating, the system works to put a halt to the denial and bingeing that result from seeing food as the enemy. Includes worksheets and exercises and lots of good information on healthy eating.

I Am Beautiful: A Celebration of Women in Their Own Words (Dana Carpenter and Woody Winfree, eds., Rose Communications, 1997, 200 pp., $27.50).

Over 500 women from all walks of life, and of all shapes, sizes, and races, talk about discovering their own beauty. Women who have conquered cancer, escaped abuse, and faced a full range of challenging human experiences tell their stories and challenge common definitions of beauty. This moving group of essays, accompanied by powerful photographs, provides a jumping-off point for mothers and teens to discuss beauty, body image, and alternatives to the unhealthy, media-driven images of girls and women.

Like Mother, Like Daughter: How Women Are Influenced by Their Mothers' Relationship with Food—and How to Break the Pattern (Debra Waterhouse, Hyperion, 1997, 232 pp., $21.95).
Written by a nutritionist, this book integrates psychology and physiology in its effort to help women understand their relationship with food and how pressure for women's and girls' unrealistic body weights is often passed down from generation to generation. Based on a respect for and understanding of the female body, the book is full of good advice about eating, dieting, and exercise, and includes a discussion about how to guide your daughter through a healthy, self-accepting transition from childhood to young womanhood.

Debra Waterhouse has a companion book called *Working as a Team to Build Body Image and Self-Esteem: A Workbook to Help Young Women Feed and Respect the Bodies They Were Born With* that can be ordered for $12.00 from:

Working as a Team
P.O. Box 4735
Portland, ME 04112

My Body, My Self for Girls: The "What's Happening to My Body?" Workbook (Lynda Madaras and Area Madaras, Newmarket Press, 1993, 128 pp., $11.95).
A companion to *What's Happening to My Body? for Girls* (see page 142), this activity book helps girls understand physical changes at puberty and encourages them to feel good about being female by celebrating the changes. Every topic imaginable is covered, from how girls feel about their first pubic hairs to how to perform a breast exam. Written for girls, it can also be a helpful book for parents to understand what girls need to know on this subject.

The Period Book: Everything You Don't Want to Ask (But Need to Know) (Karen Gravelle and Jennifer Gravelle, Walker & Co., 1996, 128 pp., $8.95).
Written by a teenage girl and her aunt, this practical book offers facts and guidance about physical, social, and emotional changes girls experience at puberty. The straightforward approach and light-

hearted illustrations make this a friendly book for pre-teen and young teenage girls.

Real Gorgeous: The Truth About Body and Beauty (Kaz Cooke, W. W. Norton, 1996, 257 pp., $13.00).
Filled with cartoons, jokes, quotes, and hard-hitting analysis of the fashion, beauty, and diet industries, this book will stimulate lots of discussion between adults and teens, as well as provide practical ideas to help readers befriend their bodies. Fat, breasts, thighs, smells, "perfection," underwear, and just about every other topic imaginable are covered in a no-punches-pulled style that lets no one off the hook. Very accessible for teen readers and a good conversation starter for teens and moms.

What's Happening to My Body? Book for Girls: A Growing Up Guide for Parents and Daughters (Lynda Madaras with Area Madaras, Newmarket Press, 1997, 304 pp., $18.95).
A bestselling classic, this book is designed to help girls and their parents understand and communicate about the changes girls experience at puberty. Covering every topic imaginable, from body hair and pimples to menstruation and dating, in clear simple language, this guide eases the discomfort most people feel about bringing up these issues. The author includes lots of examples from her own growing-up years—and other girls'—helping make the information relevant to young girls' lives.

When Girls Feel Fat: Helping Girls Through Adolescence (Sandra Susan Friedman, Harper Collins, 1997, 240 pp, $20.00).
Written by a therapist whose practice emphasizes teenage girls, *When Girls Feel Fat* offers a discussion of what "I feel fat" really means, and provides strategies for dealing with worries about weight in a constructive, supportive way. Friedman is also the author of *Girls in the 90s: Helping Girls Navigate the Rocky Road Through Adolescence*, an eating-disorder prevention program designed to help women guide girls toward understanding and acceptance of themselves and the changes they experience in adolescence. (*Girls in the 90s* is available from Salal Books at 604-689-8399.)

Radiance

Radiance is the "magazine for large women" and, as part of its commitment to helping large women feel good about their size, they are involved in activities to help large girls grow up being comfortable with their size. Activities have included essay contests, resource information for youth and school programs, and special editions of the magazine for young people. In addition to its specific efforts on behalf of young people, the magazine is filled with positive role models, making it a great magazine to have around. For more information, contact:

> *Radiance* Magazine
> P.O. Box 30246
> Oakland, CA 94604
> (510) 482-0680
> www.radiancemagazine.com

The Right Moves: A Girl's Guide to Getting Fit and Feeling Good

(Tina Schwager and Michele Schuerger, Free Spirit, 1998, 276 pp., $14.95).

This book guides girls down the path to fitness and feeling good with easy-to-understand information broken into three categories: (1)"Pump Yourself Up," which is about positive-attitude building; (2)"Food Is Your Fuel," which is about smart eating and nutrition (and why diets don't work); and (3)"Bodies in Motion,"concerning fitness, sports, and finding the right exercise program.

ORGANIZATIONS AND WEB SITES

About-Face

This all-volunteer consciousness-raising organization started the Please Don't Feed the Models campaign with its clever poster of an animal-cracker box filled with starving models. This work won them national acclaim and they have gone on to produce more posters and related products (like bumper stickers that say YOUR MIND NEVER GOES OUT OF FASHION). Their other efforts include educating people about body image, the negative effects of the fashion, advertising, and entertainment industries on girls' and women's self-esteem, how to protest the trend, and how to overcome media influence. Visit their Web site to check out the Gallery of [advertising] Offenders, links to related sites, find out how to protest the portrayal of deathly thin women as the ideal, get a look at their antistarvation products, and find out how you can help support their efforts.

> About-Face
> P.O. Box 77665
> San Francisco, CA 94107
> (415) 436-0212
> www.about-face.org

Eating Disorders Awareness and Prevention, Inc.

This nonprofit organization sponsors a national network of volunteers and state and local coordinators around the country in an effort to develop public awareness about the number of people suffering from eating disorders, and to educate people about prevention. Brochures, posters, buttons, and other resource materials are available for use in community-awareness efforts. The organization sponsors Annual Eating Disorders Awareness Week in the spring of each year.

For more information, contact:

> Eating Disorders Awareness and Prevention, Inc.
> 603 Stewart St., Suite 803
> Seattle, WA 98101
> (206) 382-3587
> http://members.aol.com/edapinc

Council on Size and Weight Discrimination

This organization works to influence public policy and opinion with the goal of ending discrimination based on body size, shape, or weight. The council offers referral services, a bibliography on eating disorders and size issues, access to its database of professionals and health-care workers who are members of the International No Diet Coalition, and education programs. Their Kids Come In All Sizes program is designed to help large children accept themselves and educate others about size discrimination and its effects on everyone. Eating decisions, eating disorders, bulimia, and other topics affecting pre-teen and teenage girls are covered.

For more information and a list of learning materials and bibliographies, contact:

Council on Size and Weight Discrimination
P.O. Box 305
Mt. Marion, NY 12456
(914) 679-1209

Media Watch

A watch-dog organization that keeps its eye on the media and reports on abusive, stereotypical images, Media Watch offers many resources to help girls understand and evaluate the ways their self-esteem, body image, and goals can be affected by the news and entertainment industries. To get a quick taste of their educational materials and the flavor of their commentary, and to review their top "worst" stories, visit their Web site.

For more information, contact:
Media Watch
P.O. Box 618
Santa Cruz, CA 95061
(408) 423-6355
www.mediawatch.com

National Eating Disorders Organization (NEDO)

NEDO's mission is to increase understanding and prevention of eating disorders through education, research, and a national and international referral network. The organization offers a variety of services and products, including an information hot line, referral services for people seeking treatment or support groups, and a variety of publications and information packets about support groups, treatment, and warning signs. NEDO is also affiliated with an organization, Anorexia Nervosa Related Eating Disorders (ANRED), whose sole function is to maintain an extensive eating disorders Web site at www.anred.com.

For more information, contact:
National Eating Disorders Organization
6655 South Yale Ave.
Tulsa, OK 74136
(918) 481-4044
www.laureate.com

Women Insisting on Natural Shapes (WINS)

WINS is a nonprofit organization working to change the image of women in media and advertising to normal diverse images, and to educate girls and women about what healthy, normal female shapes are and about the dangers of dieting and eating disorders. The WINS newsletter is an educational read, covering companies that offer realistic products for women and girls and feature articles on topics from exercise to enjoying summer despite bathing suit phobias. Lots of good grist for parent-daughter discussions.

For more information, contact:
Women Insisting on Natural Shapes (WINS)
P.O. Box 19938
Sacramento, CA 95819
(800) 600-9467

BUSINESS AND FINANCE

In addition to the resources below, be sure to review the programs described in "National Organizations" on page 174, which include exciting opportunities like She's on the Money: Economic Literacy for Girls, offered by Girls Incorporated.

BOOKS

Girls and Young Women Entrepreneurs: True Stories About Starting and Running a Business (Frances A. Karnes and Suzanne Bean, Free Spirit, 1997, 200 pp., $12.95).
This three-part book starts with young female entrepreneurs telling their own stories, describing how they conceived their businesses and what they did to get them started and keep them going. Part two includes a step-by-step guide for becoming an entrepreneur, and part three includes profiles of successful women business owners and a list of organizations to contact for help and information.

No More Frogs to Kiss: 99 Ways to Give Economic Power to Girls (Joline Godfrey, Harper, 1995, 215 pp., $12.00).
A guide to getting girls started on the path to economic self-reliance, this book provides specific activity ideas, like how to start a small home business, shop for good deals, and start a saving plan. Suc-

cessful girl entrepreneurs with businesses that range from the traditional to the wildly imaginative are profiled. Statistics about women are used throughout to reinforce the profiles and activity ideas. A directory of organizations, a glossary of business terms, and a reading list are also included.

MAGAZINES

Kid's *Wall Street News*

If you have a budding financial wizard or if you just want to encourage your daughter's awareness of finance and business, this magazine offers lots of ways to hook readers in to what many might think is a dry topic. Profiles of people in business (many of whom have a social cause they're working for) and kids and teens who have started businesses, articles about how inflation works (and why it might mean readers should consider negotiating a raise in their allowances!), and similar topics make the world of high finance interesting and lively. For more information, contact:

> Kids' *Wall Street News*
> P.O. Box 1207
> Rancho Santa Fe, CA 92067
> (800) 998-5400
> www.kwsnews.com

ORGANIZATIONS, CAMPS, AND WEB SITES

Independent Means (IMI)

Founded by Joline Godfrey, businesswoman and author of the groundbreaking *Our Wildest Dreams: Women Entrepreneurs, Making Money, Having Fun, Doing Good,* this organization promotes girls' economic self-sufficiency and offers products and services in support of that mission. IMI sponsors a national business plan contest, conferences where girls can meet women entrepreneurs, and a school program satellite broadcast called Picture Yourself in Business. It also runs a girls' entrepreneurship camp called Camp $tart-Up and develops and markets fun learning materials. In addition to information about its programs, IMI's Web site is packed with information to help girls understand business and finance, from "Independence Hall," which features articles by Joline Godfrey about money management and financial savvy to "Just Ask Her," where girls can send their E-mail questions to business owners. A teen-business-page directory, links to other sites, and "News and Info" are also included. For more information, contact:

Independent Means
126 Powers Ave.
Santa Barbara, CA 93103
(800) 350-2978 (recorded information and materials request about girls' business programs)
(800) 350-1816 (live person)
www.independentmeans.com

The Fund for Social Entrepreneurs

This program is not just for girls and young women, but offers an important resource for young women with an entrepreneurial inclination who also would like to base a business enterprise on development of a nonprofit youth-service organization. Research has shown that many women entrepreneurs start businesses out of a desire to lend support to an issue they believe in. Some are for-profit ventures like Anita Roddick's Body Shop, and others are not-for-profit ventures, like Joline Godfrey's Independent Means. For young women who want to follow in these footsteps, the fund can offer a starting point. After an annual search, five to seven entrepreneurs are selected for a two-year assistance program that offers financial support, training, consulting, and mentorship. The organization's Web site provides in-depth information about the program and profiles past recipients and their ventures.

For more information, contact:

The Fund for Social Entrepreneurs
Youth Service America
1101 15th St. NW
Suite 200
Washington, DC 20005
(202) 296-2992
www.ysa.org

KidsWay

KidsWay provides information and learning opportunities about business, careers, finance, and entrepreneurship for young people ages eight to eighteen. Their magazine, *Young Entrepreneur*, features real kids in business and includes all the information and tips needed to get kids started on their own ventures. KidsWay sponsors entrepreneurship clubs and camps and offers a fun Web site where kids can take entrepreneurship and finance quizzes, find out what other young entrepreneurs are doing, and order a catalog of books and business learning resources.

For more information, contact:

(888) KIDSWAY
www.kidsway.com

Mother and Daughter Entrepreneurs in Team (MADE-IT)

This pilot program to encourage girls and their mothers to share an entrepreneurial interest is offered in several spots around the country. Designed for young teens (ages thirteen and fourteen) and their mothers, this program provides the knowledge and skills needed to identify and initiate a business enterprise. Also included is guidance about how to have a healthy, productive relationship as business partners. For more information and to see if there is program in your area, contact:

MADE-IT
Kauffman Center for Entrepreneurial Leadership
Ewing Marion Kauffman Foundation
4900 Oak St.
Kansas City, MO 64112
(816) 932-1402
www.emkf.org

The National Education Center for Women in Business

This organization conducts research about women and business ownership, and provides entrepreneurship and business training targeted to women. As a part of those efforts, it also offers programs for girls. Camp Entrepreneur Adventure is an introductory program that introduces girls to entrepreneurship with computer simulations, budgeting, market planning, talking with successful women business owners, and other activities. Camp Entrepreneur Executive is designed for the daughters of family-business owners to prepare them for involvement and succession. The camps are offered at college campuses around the country. The center's Web site offers information about the camps and is a fun place to visit, with an on-line entrepreneur-aptitude quiz, profiles of successful businesswomen, and information about NECWB's research activities. For more information, contact:

> The National Education Center for Women in Business
> Seton Hill Drive
> Greenburg, PA 15601
> (800) NECWB-4U
> www.necwb.setonhill.edu

The National Council on Economic Education

The council develops teaching material that they describe as "designed to provide teachers with tools to help students think, choose and function in a changing global economy." Many involve real-life simulations, like getting a paycheck and "spending" it on bills, groceries, and rent. One girl said she learned a lot because it was "educational in a fun way." Check to see if these, or similar, resources are available in your daughter's school and, if not, suggest that they might be appropriate.

For a catalog of materials, which includes a list of affiliated state councils, and for more information, contact:

> National Council on Economic Education
> 1140 Avenue of the Americas
> New York, NY 10036
> (800) 338-1192

Junior Achievement

Junior Achievement offers targeted learning opportunities for middle and high-school students through its national volunteer training program, with an emphasis on preparation for economic and career decision-making. Personal Economics, Enterprise in Action, Company Program, and Globe (an international trade and business program) are just a few of the interactive learning programs available. Check to see if any of these programs are available in your daughter's school. Also consider becoming a volunteer and receiving training through Junior Achievement.

For more information, contact:

> Junior Achievement
> One Education Way
> Colorado Springs, CO 80906
> (719) 540-8000
> www.ja.org

The listings in this section include information about resources, like the list of girls' Web sites, that will help your daughter get comfortable in the world of high-tech even if she's not a whiz and doesn't have an interest in a related career. Resources specifically to foster math and science as careers are also included. Also check "National Organizations" (page 174) and "Gender Equity, Feminism, and Equal Rights" on page 163 for information about additional programs and resources. In this resources list, specifically check the Web site Expect the Best from a Girl (www.academic.org), which has some great tips for encouraging girls in math and science and a list of science camps and learning opportunities for girls. The Web site for the American Association of University Women (www.aauw.org) also has links to other valuable sites, like Tap Junior, a Web site of links to math, science, and technology sites, whose own address is so long it's faster to visit by linking from the AAUW site. *New Moon* magazine (see page 173) also offers lots of good videos and books to encourage girls in science and math, and it is always reviewing the latest publications.

BOOKS

Cool Careers for Girls in Computers (Ceel Pasternak and Linda Thornburg, Impact Publishing, 1999, 125 pp., $12.95).
Written for girls up to about the age of fourteen, this book will help the computer-savvy girl focus her interests, as well as help girls who are not very interested in computers understand the wealth of interesting and varied opportunities in the field. Readers will meet real women who work with computers every day, and get a picture of what personality traits and mental abilities are needed for careers from software engineer, Web master, and systems analyst to database manager. A personality checklist, salary information, and a list of helpful organizations is included.

Does Jane Compute?: Preserving Our Daughters' Place in the Cyber Revolution (Roberta Furger, Warner Books, 1998, 210 pp., $10.99).
If you have any doubt that there is a gender gap in computer literacy

among girls and boys—and men and women—and that the gap can spell economic hardship for your daughter as she moves into the world of work, read this book. While the picture painted by the author is distressing, she offers resources and strategies for getting girls involved and interested in computers and computing. Stories and anecdotes of classrooms and camps, along with conversations the author had with girls, bring home the need to address the issues of girls' access to and use of computers.

Girls and Young Women Inventing: Twenty True Stories About Inventors, Plus How You Can Be One Yourself (Frances A. Karnes and Suzanne Bean, Free Spirit Publishing, 1995, 176 pp., $12.95). Twenty successful teen and young women entrepreneurs tell their own stories of how they thought of their ideas and the steps they took to turn them into real products. Readers get an inside picture of the ingenuity, persistence, and enjoyment of problem-solving shared by all the inventors. A step-by-step guide for developing ideas is included for girls who want to try their hand at inventing, along with a section on organizations young inventors can turn to for help. Profiles of successful women inventors are also included.

Tech Girl's Internet Adventures (Girl Tech Team, IDG Books Worldwide, 1997, 178 pp., $19.99).
This is a great book to use to get girls interested in and started on the Internet. Jam-packed with information and activities, it walks girls through the first steps of getting on-line and then takes them on a whirlwind tour of Web sites that are educational and fun. Girls can learn about women inventors, visit on-line art galleries, check out museums all over the world, and take a look at Web sites created by girls just like them. (The book comes with a CD-ROM that includes software for creating a home page.) Check for a companion book, *Tech Girl's Activity Book*, which was being written at press time.

Twentieth-Century Women Scientists (Lisa Yount, Facts on File, 1996, 123 pp., $16.95).
This book of short biographies of ten modern women scientists pulls readers into each story with a compelling initial anecdote. For example, the biography of Rita Levi-Montalcini, who discovered nerve

growth factor, begins with a story of a woman who suffers from Alzheimer's and a young man who has been in a wheelchair since a motorcycle accident, then goes on to describe how Montalcini's work is being used to help people like this. This approach—which makes it clear that science is connected to everyday life—offers an important perspective for all girls, whether they are interested in a science career or not.

WEB SITES AND SOFTWARE

In addition to the Web sites listed here, be sure to visit the Web sites sponsored by girls' magazines (page 172), many of the national organizations (page 174), and ones in each of the topic categories that interests you, like "Sports and Physical Activities" or "Body Image and Media Representation of Women." The number of sites for girls is growing by leaps and bounds and since I can only include a limited number here, I've chosen ones that have been around for a while and look like they're going to endure. The beauty of these sites is their inclusion of links to other great and late-breaking sites; even if a great site is not on this list, you'll be able to visit it by using the links on the sites below.

The Web sites below for companies that produce software are included here because their development process is based on research about girls and focus groups conducted with them. The founders of these companies (GirlTech, Her Interactive, and Purple Moon) are all women who come from high-tech backgrounds and have researched what, why, and how most girls begin to get involved with computers. In general, their results show that girls want to explore with computers many of the things they want to explore in the nonvirtual world: relationships and communication. As a result, much of the software designed for girls emphasizes these topics and offers an avenue for girls to enter the world of high technology by using it as a tool to support their interests.

FeMiNa

This site is the equivalent of Yahoo! and other sites that catalog Web resources, but it focuses strictly on resources for women and girls. It has a whole section for girls that includes links to sites about books and magazines, camps, careers, games and activities, health, music, sports, pageants and scholarships. If your daughter is looking for

153

interesting things to become involved in, this is a great place to start on the Web. Or if you're looking for educational experiences for her, parenting advice, or just about anything related to women and girls, you'll find help at www.femina.com.

G.I.R.L.

This site, which stands for Girls Internationally Writing Letters, was started by a young teenage girl as a way to help girls find international pen pals—or should we say E-pals? Along with hooking up girls eight to fourteen around the globe, G.I.R.L. has lots of other fun on-line activities, including a girl's bulletin board, a suggestion spot, and places for girls to post their writing. It also includes fun links and ideas for girls who want to design their own Web site. Take a look at www.worldkids.net/girl.

Girl Games and Planet Girl

Girl Games is a software publisher and host of Planet Girl, a fun interactive Web site for girls. The company's premier software program, Let's Talk About Me, was one of the first to give girls what they said they wanted: something that allowed them to jump back and forth easily between different activities (like writing in a diary or planning their wardrobe), and that emphasized relationships, not shoot-'em-ups. Planet Girl features lots of interactive fun for girls, like on-line games, electronic postcards, and Girls Interwire, where girls can read and write about important issues in their lives. Visit the Web sites at www.girlgames.com or www.planetgirl.com.

Girls Place

Girls Place is inhabited by "cyber-girls" who face the same kinds of situations real girls face every day, giving visitors an opportunity to explore their feelings about relationships, money, education, family, and other important topics. One spot on the site, Our World, lets girls write about their own experiences and share them with other Web visitors. Check them out at www.girlsplace.com.

GirlSite

This site calls itself a "community of girls on the Net," and lives up to that description with a place where girls can learn about topics of interest, like career choices (experts answer girls' questions), a place to share poetry, stories, photography, opinions, information about community service projects, and other activities. Password-protected chat rooms and electronic bulletin boards offer lots of opportunities for girls to share their ideas and feelings with their peers at www.girlsite.com.

Girl Tech

From the same people who developed the book *Tech Girls*, described above. Girl Tech's mission is to get girls and young women involved in technology, math and science, and other domains, like leadership, that are often mostly populated by men. The site encourages girls to be whatever they want to be and provides resources and encouragement for accomplishing their goals. Girl Tech also publishes software and invents electronic products based on research with girls. Visit their site at www.girltech.com.

GirlZone

GirlZone has lots of great stuff for girls to explore, including book reviews by other girls, information about health and fitness (called Bodyopolis), ways to work for a cause, profiles of girls from around the globe, career information, and chat rooms. Take a look at www.girlzone.com.

gURL

gURL is a hip feminist site for girls that encourages them to think about how women and girls are treated in our culture and to control their lives and environment. Chat rooms where girls can express themselves and find out what other girls are thinking are available. The site also includes lots of girls' writing and hosts girls' Web sites for free. Software and tips for creating a home page are included. Check it out at www.gurl.com.

InGear

The main purpose of this site, which stands for Integrating Gender Equity Reform, is to encourage girls in math and science by serving as a clearinghouse. Hundreds of links to sites describing programs and resources are included. Many of the programs described are geared to teachers, but there are some gems for girls, particularly older ones who are considering science as a career and want guidance. The address is www.coe.uga.edu/ingear/.

Her Interactive

This site and software publisher go by the catchphrase "for girls who aren't afraid to use a mouse." Their CD-ROM software features strong female protagonists and stresses problem-solving. In The Vampire Diaries a high-school student goes sleuthing to find out why children are disappearing in her sleepy little town. Logic, persistence, and a good understanding of people are required skills to solve the mystery. In McKenzie & Company a group of high-school girls need to make important decisions about their family, social, and academic lives—and more when they pool their money to buy a car, dubbed "McKenzie." The Web site, where girls can go to learn about the software and participate in on-line activities, includes a password-protected area called Female Web Solutions for girls who want to learn more about, and become involved in, Internet and World Wide Web activities. Visit the Web site at www.herinteractive.com.

Purple Moon

Purple Moon is another software publisher whose efforts are research-based—even down to the name and selection of the color purple, which was a favorite pick by girls. Purple Moon's CD-ROM software programs are adventure games for pre-teen and very early teenage girls that feature the same group of girls in every adventure. The girls are "real," with their own personalities and foibles, and come in different colors and sizes. The company's Web site features lots of information about their products and the girls who appear in the games, along with other fun stuff for girls to do, like sending electronic postcards, entering contests, and giving Purple Moon feedback about its products and Web site. Take a look at www.purple-moon.com.

SmartGirl

SmartGirl is a site where girls can go to talk; learn; find answers to questions; read (and write) reviews of books, software, movies, and music; speak out on issues they care about; and get advice on questions about school, parents, money, harassment, and other important topics. Visit with other smart girls at www.smartgirl.com.

ORGANIZATIONS

Advocates for Women in Science, Engineering and Mathematics (AWSEM)

AWSEM offers an exciting array of activities and resources to encourage girls in math, science, and related careers. Started as a local and statewide mentoring program in Oregon, the organization has expanded to other locations and a partnership with Women in Technology International to increase its mentorship program. AWSEM sponsors a poster contest by girls on the subject of women in science and makes the exhibition available to schools and organizations. To get a good picture of what AWSEM offers, a visit to their Web site is a must. You'll find science activity ideas, links to lots of related sites and resources, ideas for getting your daughter involved in math and science, and more.

For more information, contact:

Advocates for Women in Science, Engineering and
   Mathematics (AWSEM)
P.O. Box 91000
Portland, OR 97291
(503) 690-1261
www.awsem.org

Connections Across Cultures

This fascinating program, supported by the National Science Foundation, was developed out of the realization that while girls, Native Americans, Hispanics, and African Americans make up over 50 percent of the student population, their participation in math, science, and technology courses is much lower. Program developers asked if there are commonalities in the ways these groups think and problem-solve that might provide insight into developing programs to attract them to these fields. The answer was yes, and the program, which promotes social interaction, open-ended discovery and problem-solving, and an exploration of the role of technology in society, is being implemented in classrooms around the country. While the program is still small, the goal is to increase the number of classrooms, so check to see if there is one in your area. An informative booklet about the background and development of this program is available for free.

157

For more information, or for a free booklet, contact:
National Science Foundation Pac-TEC Project
Mission College, MS-18
3000 Mission College Blvd.
Santa Clara, CA 95054
(408) 748-2764
pactec@wvmdccd.cc.ca.us

Equals Program

This program was developed at the Lawrence Hall of Science at Berkeley to increase girls' participation in math—and to increase the participation of other groups whose ethnic or economic status is sometimes correlated with limited success in math. The Equals Program encourages math by emphasizing problem-solving and interaction with others, and by using hands-on materials. In addition to classroom programs, a special "Family Math" curriculum is offered that helps adults and kids enjoy math together. As a result of its Family Math class leadership workshops, the program is offered in almost every state.

For more information about the program, and for a list of organizations offering Family Math, contact:
Equals Program
Lawrence Hall of Science
University of California
Berkeley, CA 94720
(510) 642-1823

The Math/Science Network

This network is made up of educators, parents, scientists, mathematicians, leaders in government, and members of the nonprofit and corporate sector who want to encourage girls and women to become involved in the math, science, and technology fields. To encourage girls' participation, the network sponsors a class called Expanding Your Horizons in Science, Mathematics and Engineering, which is held in over 120 locations around the country. Since this workshop was first started in 1976, more than 390,000 girls and young women have participated. The workshop, led by women scientists, emphasizes hands-on activities and is designed to make math and science learning fun and relevant to girls' lives. Career awareness information is also included.

For more information, contact:
Math/Science Network
Mills College
5000 MacArthur Blvd.
Oakland, CA 94613
(510) 430-2222
www.elstad.com/msngoal.html

Science-By-Mail

This program, sponsored by the Museum of Science in Boston, Massachusetts, gets kids involved in science no matter what their local resources might be. Designed for kids in the fourth through the ninth grades, participants work in small teams with the activity packets provided by the museum and communicate with real scientist "pen pals" by phone, E-mail, fax, or snail mail—whichever the kids choose. Scientists involved in the program donate their time and have at least a bachelor's degree in science. Members of the Association for Women in Science participate as pen pals. Though not designed just for girls, this program offers a great way to encourage your daughter in the sciences. Help her get a group of friends together for some fun and learning.

For more information, contact:
Science-By-Mail
P.O. Box 6080
Boston, MA 02212
(800) 729-3300
www.mos.org/mos/sbm/sciencemail.html

The International Women's Air and Space Museum

This museum has a great Web site girls can visit to find out about women's contributions to aviation, from Amelia Earhart to astronaut Sally Ride and other NASA astronauts. Biographies, background information, and a list of barriers broken by women in aviation—like American Jacqueline Cochrane and French pilot Jacqueline Auriol, who both broke the sound barrier—make this an inspiring spot to visit.

Check out their Web site or contact them at:
The International Women's Air and Space Museum
1507 N. Marginal Rd.
Cleveland, OH 44114
(216) 623-1111
www.iwasm.org

CAREER AND WORK

The resources included here will get you started exploring options with your daughter and steering her toward experiences that will encourage her to think about her future and economic independence. In addition to the resources in this list, be sure to check out the Web site Expect the Best from a Girl (www.academic.org) in the "Gender Equity, Feminism, and Equal Rights" resource listings (page 163) for special programs and camps for girls in subjects from career development and leadership to math, music, and science.

BOOKS

Career Choices (Mindy Bingham and Sandy Stryker, Academic Innovations, 1997, 288 pp., $22.95).
By the authors of *Choices*, described on page 126, this guide helps girls understand who they are, what they want out of life, and how to integrate that information with career choices. The interactive approach includes exercises and activities that will help teens envision their future and design a plan to help them get there. (The publisher has a variety of related materials and books. They can be contacted at www.academicinnovations.com or 805-967-8015.)

Images: A Career Preparation Workbook for Black Students (Mattie Evans Gray, California Department of Education, 186 pp., $10.00).
This is a workbook-style guide for black girls in sixth through twelfth grades, designed to help them think about career options and the academic achievements required to achieve their goals. Profiles of successful role models who share their stories and insights are included, as well as step-by-step activities. Order this book from Advocacy Press (800-676-1480) or Resources for Girls and Young Women (805-569-2398).

Girls Seen and Heard: 52 Lessons for Our Daughters (The Ms. Foundation and Sandra Forsyth, Putnam, 1998, 224 pp., $11.95). Based on the successful Take Our Daughters to Work Day, which is sponsored by the Ms. Foundation, this book offers a smorgasboard of ideas and discussion topics for girls and adults. Filled with short, punchy chapters on topics ranging from having a dream, why sports are good for girls, and why playing dumb is stupid to self-defense, *Girls Seen and Heard* will inspire and motivate girls to take an active role in controlling their futures. Also included is a reading list, resource directory, and interactive ideas for encouraging girls' participation.

Mariposa: A Workbook for Discovery and Exploration for Young Latinas (Maria Elena Fernandez, California Department of Education, 246 pp., $19.95).

This activity-based book is designed to encourage Latinas to dream about career options and develop the leadership and decision-making skills required to achieve those dreams. The interactive workbook approach fosters pride in their roots and addresses unique challenges they may face. Order this book from Advocacy Press (800-676-1480) or Resources for Girls and Young Women (805-569-2398).

Women and Work: In Their Own Words (Maureen Michelson, ed., New Sage Press, 1994, 109 pp., $14.95).

This collection of stories about women from diverse cultural backgrounds in all walks of life, from judge to coal miner, gives girls an inside look at the rewards and challenges facing working women in our society. Photographs are included with each biographical sketch.

Organizations and Web Sites

Take Our Daughters to Work Day

The Ms. Foundation sponsors Take Our Daughters to Work Day the last Thursday of April each year. As *the* day when people are aware that daughters are visiting workplaces all across the country, this is an exciting event to participate in. The Ms. Foundation Web site includes information about how to contact people who are involved in planning activities for your area. (Go to the bottom of the page and click on "Contact Map.") The site also features an area called Girlworld where girls can find out about Take Your Daughter to Work Day and why it was started, and send their ideas to the Ms. Foundation.

In addition to providing information about Take Our Daughters to Work Day, the Ms. Foundation is involved in other activities to help girls and women. For more information about these activities, call their fax-back number at 800-809-8206 to request a list of free information sheets. For more information, contact:

Ms. Foundation
120 Wall St.
33rd Floor
New York, NY 10005
(800) 676-7780
www.ms.foundation.org

National Mentoring Partnership

The National Mentoring Partnership works to promote adults' involvement in young people's lives by developing partnerships with organizations to promote mentoring, coordinating efforts to reduce duplication of services, and developing innovative programs designed to bring more mentors to more children and young adults. The partnership has helped over 25,000 young people across the nation find a mentor and has set a goal of increasing that number to 2 million. A visit to their Web site will give you lots of motivation to find a mentor for your daughter. Their on-line review of data is compelling; 73 percent of students who had a mentor said the mentor helped them raise their goals and expectations; 59 percent improved their grades. All students were less likely to use alcohol and illegal drugs, and to skip school or classes. The Web site also has a list of its regional offices across the country.

For more information, contact:

The National Mentoring Partnership
1400 I St., NW
Suite 850
Washington, DC 20005
(202) 729-4340
www.mentoring.org

The National School-to-Work Learning and Information Center

The center primarily serves educators, but it also offers lots of good information for parents and girls. The Web site is a valuable place to visit with your daughter because it includes quotes and stories from teens who have participated in school-to-work experiences. Also of interest is data about benefits of the programs and a listing of programs in each state.

For more information, contact:

The National School-to-Work Learning and Information Center
400 Virginia Ave.
Suite 210
Washington, DC 20024
(800) 251-7236
www.stw.ed.gov

GENDER EQUITY, FEMINISM, AND EQUAL RIGHTS

This listing is an eclectic mix of information about resources that celebrate women's contributions and accomplishments, as well as ones intended to educate about the continuing need to ensure equal opportunities for, and equal treatment of, women and girls. For books and other resources that portray accomplished women in specific subject areas, like science or sports, check the resource listings for those categories.

BOOKS

The listings in this section offer lots of ways to let girls know that women have played an important role in history, that women have done—and are doing—interesting things with their lives. For books about girls' and women's participation in specific fields, check the resource listings for "Activism" (page 119), "Self-Expression" (page 179), "Math, Science, and Technology" (page 151), "Business and Finance" (page 146), and "Sports and Physical Activities"(page 183).

And Not Afraid to Dare: The Stories of Ten African American Women (Tonya Bolden, Scholastic Trade, 1998, 244 pp., $16.95). These chapter-length sketches of ten women read like fiction but let girls know in no uncertain terms that their dreams are possible.

Whether describing escaped slave Ellen Craft, Olympic gold medalist Jackie Joyner-Kersee, or writer Toni Morrison, the famous women described are all presented as real women struggling to achieve, rather than extraordinary women. In addition to the ten featured women, short biographical sketches of twenty-one other African-American women are included, along with a bibliography of suggested readings.

The Conversation Begins: Mothers and Daughters Talk about Living Feminism (Christine Looper Baker and Christine Baker Kline, Bantam Books, 1997, 387 pp., $13.95).
Twenty-two sets of feminist mothers and daughters (including the authors) discuss what feminism has meant in their lives and in the mother-daughter relationship. Included is a diverse collection of women from author Marilyn French and poet Joy Harjo to social critic Barbara Ehrenreich, health activist Barbara Seaman, and others. The variety of perspectives, backgrounds, and interests offer good jumping-off points for discussions with older teens.

Cool Women (Pamela Nelson, Girl Press, 1998, 128 pp., $19.95).
This diverse collection of fifty stories about brave women shows girls there have been "cool women" around for a long time and from all over the globe. From Cleopatra and pirates who ruled the high seas, to World War II bomber pilots and Rosie the Riveter, the profiles emphasize women who overcame their fears and defined success in their own terms regardless of the prevailing beliefs about what women should be or do.

Gender Bias Prevention Book: Helping Girls and Women to Have Satisfying Lives and Careers (Montana Katz, Jason Aronson, 1996, 360 pp., $29.95).
For parents who want to raise daughters equipped to resist limiting sexual stereotypes, this book offers insight and practical suggestions. Using an imaginary but typical girl, the author follows her development to show how gender bias operates, how it affects girls' lives and dreams, and what adults can do to counteract it. Starting with the beginnings of gender bias in early childhood, the pattern of development is followed through adulthood, including chapters on middle- and high-school experiences. Exercises and ideas for foster-

ings girls' independence and a goal orientation toward their futures are included.

Girls Who Rocked the World: Heroines from Sacajawea to Sheryl Swoopes (Amelie Welden, Beyond Words Publishing, 1998, 120 pp., $8.95).
Stories of accomplished women let girls know they can grow up to do great things, but why should they wait to grow up? This book profiles a host of girls and young women who started pursuing their dreams and accomplishing great things when they were young. Girls are introduced to historical figures like Joan of Arc and Anne Frank, and contemporary girls, like teen author S. E. Hinton, whose book *Tex* was made into a movie. Short statements by girls about their plans for rocking the world are included.

Profiles of Women Past and Present (American Association of University Women, 1996, $14.95 each volume).
Two volumes cover accomplished women in the arts, sciences, politics, and social activism. Since the book is written in the first person with lots of anecdotes, the women profiled come across as real people readers can relate to. Whether they relate to the scientist Barbara McClintock, opera singer Marian Anderson, or any of the other thirty women featured in these books, girls will come away knowing that women can do interesting and exciting things that make a difference in the world. Ideas for fun teaching activities are included.

Young Oxford History of Women in the United States (11-volume set, Oxford University Press, 1998, 144 pp. each, $9.95 each).
This set of books authored by experts in their fields covers the entire history of women in America, starting with the experience of Native American women during colonization. From that beginning, one volume covers each key period, from colonial times through the early sixties and the emergence of the women's movement. Books can be purchased individually or as a set, depending on your daughter's interests.

Voices of Feminism: Past, Present and Future (Joann Bren Guernsey, Lerner Publications, 1997, 96 pp., $9.95).
For the teen interested in learning more about feminism, this book

offers a historical overview, information about key players, and a discussion of the issues involved in the emergence and development of the movement. While everything from the suffragette movement of the 1800s to the formation of the National Association for Women is covered, the book revolves around a discussion of ideas and key figures, not chronology. Girls will be introduced to Susan B. Anthony, Betty Friedan, Gloria Steinem, and others who have been influential in supporting women's rights, as well as people who have fought against their efforts.

Gloria Steinem: Feminist Extraordinaire (Caroline Lazo, Lerner Publications, 1998, 128 pp., $23.00).
This biography for young people chronicling Steinem's life covers her difficult childhood, her college years at Smith, her travels in India, her first work as a journalist in New York, her pivotal role in the early feminist movement, and the founding of *Ms.* magazine and the National Women's Political Caucus. Steinem becomes real through this account of her dreams and struggles, offering girls inspiration as well as a history lesson in feminism.

Failing at Fairness: How Our Schools Cheat Girls (Myra and David Sadker, Scribner's, 1994, 347 pp., $12.00).
Based on thousands of hours of classroom observation of teachers, girls, and boys, *Failing at Fairness* reveals an alarming level of un-intentional gender bias in our classrooms. The Sadkers found that boys get more help from teachers because "they need it more." Girls see few, if any, influential women presented in their textbooks. Boys can shout out answers in class with impunity; girls cannot. Through examples like these and a discussion of research findings, the book offers a compelling look at how different girls' and boys' experience of school is, and the kinds of changes needed to eliminate bias.

School Girls: Young Women, Self-Esteem and the Confidence Gap (Peggy Orenstein, Anchor, 1995, 335 pp., $14.00).
Journalist Peggy Orenstein, struck by discouraging data about adolescent girls' drop in self-esteem and confidence, spent a year following girls in several California schools as they went about their lives at school, at home, and in social and extracurricular activities. Read-

ers meet smart girls who deliberately play dumb in math class, girls who are harassed by boys but are afraid to speak up about it, teachers who don't see that they are calling on boys much more frequently than girls or reprimanding girls for behavior accepted by boys. The picture of girls—as they try to understand and fit into their idea of what it means to be a girl and a woman in our society—that emerges from these accounts and others should be required reading for all parents and teachers.

ORGANIZATIONS AND WEB SITES

Advocacy Press

The publishing arm of the Santa Barbara Girls Incorporated office, Advocacy Press offers an excellent collection of materials for children, teens, and adults designed to foster gender equity and career and life planning. Books, videos, workbooks, and training programs are available. Just reviewing their catalog is an eye-opener; there are many good books and learning materials available to help parents and adults foster girls' self-esteem and confidence. Find out what is current and what is working by requesting a catalog and ordering some of their books. The catalog is also valuable for giving you a picture of the Choices life and career planning programs used in Girls Incorporated centers around the country.

For a catalog or more information, contact:

Advocacy Press
P.O. Box 236
Santa Barbara, CA 93102
(800) 676-1480

Girls Count

This organization provides parents, educators, policy makers, and business leaders with tools to ensure that girls grow up with a world of possibilities for their lives and futures. They offer a variety of training programs and materials appropriate for educators and parents, including Parenting Our Daughters, a program that guides parents in helping girls overcome sex stereotyping, expand their horizons, and increase their involvement in education.

For more information, contact:

Girls Count
225 E. 16th Ave.
Suite 475
Denver, CO 80203
(303) 832-7331
www.girlscount.org

Expect the Best from a Girl. That's What You'll Get.
This Web site, a joint effort of Mount Holyoke College, the Women's College Coalition, and the Ad Council, is a gold mine of ideas and resources for parents who want to encourage their daughters to achieve and pursue interesting careers. It includes resource information, practical ideas for helping girls, and listings of workshops and camps around the country for girls in entrepreneurship, leadership, science, writing, art, and a myriad of other subjects. If you're looking for interesting and challenging opportunities for your daughter, visit this site (www.academic.org). For a free pamphlet from the sponsors that includes lots of practical suggestions about how to encourage your daughter's independence and confidence, and information about national and regional programs, call 800-922-4447.

Feminist.com
This site (www.feminist.com) is a great place to visit for two reasons. First, it lets girls see firsthand just how much energy and effort is going into making the world a place where women and girls are safe and respected. Second, if you and your daughter are looking for information about any topic related to women, this site should be one of your first visits. The introductory page has an easy-to-use listing of search categories so it's quick to find information on topics of interest. And the topics are diverse, including women's health, business, the arts, politics, and social change—the list goes on and on. Also included is information about services in your local area, upcoming events, and interviews with influential women, like Gloria Steinem.

The Feminist Majority Leadership Internship
The Feminist Majority is a nonprofit research and advocacy organization that works for political, economic, and social change. This

organization's feminist think tank, the Feminist Majority Foundation, sponsors leadership internships for older teens and young adults (not just women) interested in being leaders in the feminist and equal rights movement. Candidates who have already worked on issues in their communities are preferred.

For more information about the internship and the organization's activities, contact:

The Feminist Majority
1600 Wilson Blvd.
Suite 801
Arlington, VA 22209
(703) 522-2219
www.feminist.org

National Council for Research on Women

The council is an alliance of organizations and individuals involved in feminist research, advocacy, program development, and policy analysis with the goal of improving the condition of women and girls. The status of girls has been a significant focus of the organization, and in 1998 it published *The Girls Report: What We Know About Growing Up Female*. A review of existing data, along with a discussion of effective programs and strategies for promoting girls' healthy development, the report offers insight and guidance for anyone interested in helping girls flourish. To order a copy of the report and for more information about the council's activities, contact:

National Council for Research on Women
11 Hanover Square, 20th Floor
New York, NY 10005
(212) 785-7335
www.ncrw.org

National Organization for Women (NOW)

NOW is a political and social action organization working on all fronts to improve the quality of women's lives, from reproduction rights and affirmative action to violence against women and global feminism. NOW has a young feminists' component, holds Young Feminist Summits, and encourages girls and young women to start chapters in their schools and communities.

For more information, contact:

National Organization for Women
P.O. Box 96824
Washington, DC 20090
(202) 331-0066
www.now.org

National Women's History Project

This organization celebrates women's accomplishments and works to educate people about the important role women have played in our country's history. The project offers educational training and workshops and sponsors special events, like Women's Equality Day and National Women's History Month. Girls with an interest in history can subscribe to the Women's History Network and receive a newsletter about what's going on in the field of women's history. Everyone should request a catalog of books, videos, posters, and other neat products like sweatshirts, balloons, pens, and pins that celebrate women's history. You can order the catalog by logging on to their Web site, where you can also learn more about history project activities and take an on-line history quiz. For more information, contact:

National Women's History Project
7738 Bell Road
Windsor, CA 95492
(707) 838-6000
www.nwhp.org

Marymount Institute for the Education of Women and Girls

The institute sponsors workshops and conferences for educators, parents, and girls; consults with schools and educators; works to affect public policy; and develops materials to increase awareness of gender issues. The *Equity Newsletter*, which you get as part of a modest annual membership fee, is a great resource for parents interested in keeping up on issues and resources for helping girls grow up smart and confident. Book reviews, a national calendar of events, interviews with experts, and news briefs on interesting products and events ensure a steady stream of useful information.

For more information, contact:
> Marymount Institute for the Education of Women and Girls
> Marymount College Tarrytown
> 100 Marymount Ave.
> Tarrytown, NY 10591
> (914) 332-4917

Resources for Girls and Young Women
This organization is a great one-stop-shopping place for books and other publications designed to build girls' self-esteem, help girls in career and life planning, and encourage participation in math and science. Training in use of the materials and gender-equity issues is available for small and large groups. For more information, contact:
> Resources for Girls and Young Women
> 817 Vincente Way
> Santa Barbara, CA 93105
> (805) 569-2398

WEEA Resource Center
WEEA stands for Women's Educational Equity Act, and this group's resource center offers information, publications, and guidance for parents, educators, and policy makers interested in gender-equity issues, including sexual harassment, violence against girls and women, equal educational opportunities, girls' participation in math and science, and a host of related issues. To keep up to date on information on these topics, you can subscribe to *WEEA Digest On-line*, which will send you information about interesting research and publications to be downloaded or ordered by snail mail. A visit to the resource center's Web site is a great way to get an overview of what they offer.
For more information, contact
> WEEA Resource Center
> The Educational Development Center
> 55 Chapel St.
> Newton, MA 02458
> (800) 225-3088
> www.edc.org/womensequity

MAGAZINES FOR GIRLS

Lots of magazines for girls and young women encourage them to buy into many of our cultural myths: Thin is better, or should we say best. Girls and women are defined by the male company they keep. Makeup and clothes make the woman. Parents will be glad to know that there are lots of alternatives to this standard fare.

American Girl

American Girl, designed for the pre-teen and young teen girl, is a playful, lively publication with profiles of "happening" girls (like inventors and authors), and articles about things on girls' minds, like friendship and school. The magazine solicits ideas and information from girls for its article topics. Pictures of girls who have contributed are often included, letting readers know that the ideas, fears, activities, and bad (or best) experiences included are from real girls. Developed by the makers of a line of historically accurate dolls and books about girls in American history, each issue features a story about an American girl from the past.

For more information, contact:

American Girl magazine
Pleasant Company Publications
8400 Fairway Place
Middleton, WI 53562
(800) 234-1278
www.americangirl.com

HUES

HUES, which stands for Hear Us Emerging Sisters and describes itself as a magazine for women of all cultures and sizes, was founded by three young women who wanted a magazine that represented and covered issues for *real* girls and young women, in all their colors, sizes, sexual persuasions, and ethnic affiliations. Articles, poems, reviews, and resources revolve around one theme in each quarterly issue. Photos and illustrations emphasize beautiful girls and young women in all their variety. Thought-provoking articles and a deliberately inclusive tone make this a great magazine for older teens.

For more information, contact:

HUES
P.O. Box 3620
Duluth, MN 55803
800-HUES-4U2
www.hues.net

New Girl Times

This publication, which bills itself as "the only newspaper written by girls," is a newspaper with a social and political conscience featuring articles about events and organizations that affect girls' lives. Information is included in most articles to help girls follow up on the issues discussed. A pen-pal section lets girls hook up with other like-minded spirits around the United States and even in other countries, and a classified ad section includes other publications looking for teen writers and artists.

For more information, contact:

New Girl Times
215 West 84th St.
New York, NY 10024
(800) 560-7525

New Moon

New Moon, for the pre-teen and younger teen girl, is written and illustrated by girls and described by the publisher as a "magazine for girls and their dreams." It includes stories, articles, art, and poetry from girls all over the world on topics that help them resist gender inequities, explore their growth from girl to woman, and pursue each of their own unique paths in life. In addition to feature articles and stories, there are lots of quick takes, like the pen-pal section, cartoons, and letters to Luna, who provides an avenue for girls to learn what other readers are thinking. Included in each issue is a *New Moon* product catalog of books, art materials, journals, videos, and products to help girls discover and like themselves.

For more information, contact:

New Moon
P.O. Box 3587
Duluth, MN 55803
(800) 381-4743
www.newmoon.org

Teen Voices

Teen Voices is another great magazine for and by girls, but with an interesting variation on the phenomenon of girl-written magazines. *Teen Voices* has an editorial board of feminists, psychologists, teachers, and women's studies experts who guide the content to ensure its value for young readers. *Teen Voices* covers topics that affect girls' lives, such as sexual harassment, racism, sports, and eating disorders and just about everything in between. The purpose of the articles is to connect readers with a community of girls and adults committed to helping girls reach their full potential. Poetry, stories, and music, book, and Web site reviews, often with photos of the authors, complement the feature articles. For more information, contact:

> *Teen Voices*
> P.O. Box 120-127
> Boston, MA 02112
> (888) 888-TEEN
> www.teenvoices.com

NATIONAL ORGANIZATIONS

While looking for a specific group, take some time to read about the other organizations included here. Not all of them are mentioned in other chapters of the book, but they offer some great resources and ideas. The organizations are listed alphabetically.

Afro-Academic, Cultural, Technological and Scientific Olympics (ACT-SO)

ACT-SO, sponsored by the National Association for the Advancement of Colored People (NAACP), is designed to encourage and acknowledge high academic and cultural achievement by African-American high school students in the same way the African-American community recognizes sports achievement. The program involves year-long enrichment activities that culminate in an annual competition in the sciences, humanities, performing arts, and the visual arts. Local competition winners go on to compete at the national level.

For more information, contact your local NAACP office or:

> The National Association for the Advancement of Colored
>   People ACT-SO Program
> 4805 Mt. Hope Dr.

Baltimore, MD 21215
(410) 358-8900
www.naacp.org

American Association of University Women (AAUW)

AAUW is a national organization working to promote education and equity for women and girls. The association conducts research, develops innovative educational programs, offers fellowships and grants, and works to raise the public's awareness of issues affecting the quality of life for women and girls in the United States. The AAUW's groundbreaking report *Shortchanging Girls, Shortchanging America* contributed to the national effort to help girls when it documented the precipitous drop in girls' self-esteem at puberty. The association offers publications about its research, like *Growing Smart: What's Working for Girls in School* and *Hostile Hallways: The AAUW Survey on Sexual Harassment in America's Schools* that can be eye-opening and can provide guidance for parents. In addition, it develops programs like the recent Sister-to-Sister Summits, which brought together girls from around the country to discuss and learn about issues affecting their lives. To get an overview of the association's mission, activities, and publications, visit its Web site. (While you're there, check out the links to other equity organizations and fun educational sites for girls.)

For more information, contact:

American Association of University Women
1111 16th St., NW
Washington, DC 20036
(202) 785-7700
www.aauw.org

Campfire Boys and Girls

This organization was once just for girls, but in recent years it has expanded to include boys too. It is included here because it offers girls opportunities to play and learn side by side with boys in an atmosphere that promotes self-esteem and respect for each other. Contribution to community is a major focus of this organization's programs, providing constructive avenues for girls and boys to work together to improve the quality of life in their communities. Special programs are available for teens, including reasonably priced camps

175

where teen boys and girls learn about gender, race, and age issues designed to help them accept differences, understand each other, and work together.

For more information, contact:

Campfire Boys and Girls
4601 Madison Ave.
Kansas City, MI 64112
(816) 756-1950
www.campfire.org

Coalition for America's Children

This coalition, sponsored by the Benton Foundation, is a cyber-network of adults and organizations across the country working to improve the lives of American children. Their Web site offers lots of ideas for things you can do to help children in your family and community, and includes links to organizations like the National Network for Youth and Children's Express (a great Web site for your girls to visit), where you can get information and resources designed to improve girls' lives. Also included is a clickable map to help you locate child-advocacy and support organizations in your state and local area.

Coalition for America's Children
Benton Foundation
1634 Eye St. NW
Washington, DC 20006
(202) 638-5770
www.kidscampaign.org

Girls Incorporated

Girls Incorporated is a national organization committed to inspiring every girl to be *strong, smart and bold*[SM]* through educational programs and advocacy. The programs cover every aspect of girls'

---

*The similarity between "strong, smart and bold[SM]" and the title of this book was a coincidence that reinforced the importance of these characteristics for girls. In my work with my initial advisory board of teen girls, intelligence, strength, and confidence were key qualities girls identified as important. I want to thank Girls Incorporated for accepting my book title even though it was so similar to their service trademark.

lives that affect their health, well-being, educational success, and futures. Innovative programs like Friendly PEERsuasion (an anti-drug and alcohol program), She's On the Money (an economic literacy program), Operation SMART (a math, science, and technology program), just to name a few, have been offered to millions of girls around the country. The organization also has a catalog of educational materials that includes videos, books, and research and informational materials. Visit the organization's Web site to get an overview of programs and activities and to locate a Girls Incorporated program in your area. There are also fun educational activities on-line for your daughter to participate in.

For more information, contact:

Girls Incorporated
120 Wall St.
New York, NY 10015
(212) 509-2000
www.girlsinc.org

Girls Speak Out

The moving force behind this coalition came from girls who participated in Girls Speak Out workshops across the country. (For more information about these workshops, see *Girls Speak Out: Finding Your True Self* in the "Books for Girls" resource listings on page 128.) The coalition sponsored the First National Girls Conference in 1997, with the theme "Don't Deal With It. Change It!" and developed the Girls USA Plan of Action, which provided guidelines and action plans for girls, adults, and organizations interested in making the world a safe, respectful place where girls can flourish.

For information about the organization and its activities, contact:

Girls Speak Out
P.O. Box 1799
Guerneville, CA 95446
(707) 869-0829

The National Coalition of Girls' Schools

A membership organization for girls' schools across the country, the coalition develops learning materials and publishes a variety of materials to help parents and teachers improve the lives of girls. Their publications include materials on math, science, and gender equity.

177

The coalition can also provide information about the locations of girls' schools.

For a brochure of publications and for more information, contact:

The National Coalition of Girls' Schools
228 Main Street
Concord, MA 10742
(508) 287-4485
www.ncgs.org

National Council of La Raza

The council works to help Hispanics move into the economic mainstream through education, public policy advocacy, and technical assistance. Working with over 200 affiliated organizations around the country, many of the organization's activities are designed to foster youth involvement and leadership. Teens involved with the council can participate in the Youth Leaders Program, AmeriCorps volunteerism collaboration, and other specialized activities like the anti-smoking campaign Latino Youth Standing up to Joe Camel.

For more information, contact:

National Council of the La Raza
1111 19th St., NW
Suite 1000
Washington, DC 20036
(202) 785-1670
www.nclr.org

Girl Scouts of the USA

Dedicated solely to girls, this organization is committed to creating an accepting and nurturing environment where girls can build character and skills for success in the real world. In partnership with committed adults and through a myriad of challenging programs and activities, girls "discover the fun, friendship, and power of girls together." From sports skill-building clinics, anti-smoking campaigns, and community service and environmental stewardship projects to leadership activities and cultural exchange experiences, girl scouting programs foster girls' belief in their self-worth and potential as well as promote girls' social conscience, strong values, and ability to be courageous and strong. A network of regional councils and local scout leaders make scouting opportunities available across the country. The organizaton's Web site is fun to visit, with girls' on-line activities, program information, and a national listing of councils to help you get hooked up easily with scouting programs. A network of regional councils and local scout leaders make scouting opportunities available across the country. The organization's Web site is fun to visit, with girls' on-line activities, program information, and a national listing of councils to help you get hooked up easily with scouting programs.

For more information, contact:
Girl Scouts of the USA
420 Fifth Avenue
New York, NY 10018
(212) 852-8000
www.gsusa.org (corporate site), www.girlscouts.org/girls
(special site for girls)

SELF-EXPRESSION

The resources listed here will provide budding artists, writers, and performers with role models, and help them find out how they can practice and improve their craft.

For girls involved in writing and art, be sure to check out the section on magazines for girls (page 172); all the publications described are either written and illustrated entirely by girls, or include lots of girls' writing and artwork. (Even if your daughter doesn't have a subscription, encourage her to visit the magazines' Web sites. There's lots to read and learn on-line.) Many of the Web sites for girls in the "Math, Science, and Technology" listings (see page 151) also include girls' writing and art and sponsor contests in the arts.

Books

The Young Person's Guide to Becoming a Writer (Janet Gardner, Free Spirit, 1995, 184 pp., $13.95).
From how to get started writing to having a manuscript evaluated, this book gives teens a step-by-step guide to becoming a writer. Includes exercises to help them find their own style and voice, branch out with new styles, locate appropriate publishers, and prepare a manuscript for submission. Includes resources for linking up with other writers and soliciting support from adults.

Totally Private & Personal: Journaling Ideas for Girls and Young Women (Jessica Wilbur, Free Spirit, 1996, 168 pp., $8.95). Wilbur, the teenage author of this idea-packed guide for girls, offers hundreds of suggestions, tips, and examples to help girls make the journal experience meaningful and fun. For the aspiring writer or girl who needs a place to sort out what is happening in her life, this book can get her started.

ORGANIZATIONS AND WEB SITES

A Celebration of Women Writers
This organization works to increase people's awareness and understanding of the contribution women have made to writing of all kinds, from novels and poetry to history and economics and everything in between. Browsing the Web site is the best way to appreciate how prolific and diverse women writers are—and have been throughout history. Information about women authors from 3,000 B.C. through the twentieth century is included, and can be searched by country, historical period, and name. Pictures and quotes of authors are included. This site has a very long address (www.cs.cmu.edu/people/mmbt/women/writers.html), so just go to www.feminist.com, select "Women & the Arts," and click on "A Celebration of Women Writers."

Girls Know Best Writing Contest
Beyond Words Publishing holds a Girl Writer Contest each year and publishes the winners' essays in *Girls Know Best*, an annually released anthology (see page 128). Girls get to write about anything and everything that's on their minds that they think will be helpful to other girls. Winners learn all about book publishing and marketing as they communicate with their editor, make requested changes, meet deadlines, and go to book signings and interviews once the book is published.

For more information and for submission guidelines, contact:
Beyond Words Publishing
20827 NW Cornell Road
Suite 500
Hillsboro, OR 97124
(503) 531-8700
www.beyondword.com

National Assembly of State Arts Agencies

This organization is made up of arts organizations around the country committed to helping its members develop, promote, and sustain the arts in their local and regional areas, including special programs for youth. The organization's Web site has a clickable map of the country that allows you to find out what's going on in your state and locate appropriate programs for your daughter. The assembly also works specifically to promote arts programs for at-risk youth, under-served populations, and rural residents. For more information about programs in your area, contact:

> National Assembly of States Arts Agencies
> 1029 Vermont Ave., NW
> Second Floor
> Washington, DC 20005
> (202) 347-6352
> www.nasaa-arts.org

National Museum of Women in the Arts

For aspiring artists, this museum lets girls know that there were—and are—many great and influential women artists, even if they are not featured in traditional exhibits and art history books. The museum, which collects, exhibits, and researches women's art, has an extensive collection of women's art from the fifteenth through the late-twentieth centuries, all of which can be viewed on-line at the museum's Web site. The museum store features books about women artists and other gifts related to women in the arts, and an annual calendar featuring paintings by women. The museum also has a partnership with Girl Scouts of the USA and provides special materials for troops interested in learning about the world of art and women artists.

For more information, contact:

> The National Museum of Women in the Arts
> 1250 New York Ave., NW
> Washington, DC 20005
> (202) 783-5000
> www.nmwa.org

New Moon Publishing

The founders of New Moon Publishing (see pages 139 and 173) offer participatory writing workshops for girls. The workshops include lots of writing, brainstorming, and sharing in small groups, along with big doses of practical advice, inspiration, and encouragement. (New Moon founders Joe Kelly and Nancy Gruver also offer workshops on other topics related to their work with girls.)

For more information, contact:
New Moon Publishing
P.O. Box 3587
Duluth, MN 55803
(800) 381-4734

Women in Music

This organization works to promote opportunities for, and recognition of, women in the music industry through education, networking, and career development. The organization is also involved in participating in and supporting community youth programs. For girls interested in a career in music, a visit to the Web site offers lots of information about issues related to being a professional musician and links to other music sites.

For more information about the group's activities and youth programs participation, contact:
Women in Music National Network
Suite 300
31121 Mission Blvd.
Hayward, CA 94544
(510) 232-3897
www.womeninmusic.com

Women in the Realm of Computer Visual Arts, Effects and Animation

Girls and young women who are interested in making their livings in the visual arts will most likely need to use the computer as their primary tool of expression. A visit to this site offers great encouragement and opportunities for learning. Many women artists are featured, with essays about how they became involved in the arts and how they use computers in their work. Artists offer words of advice and encouragement for younger girls and women. A mentorship program is also being organized by the founder of this site. Check out the site and learn more about the mentorship programs at www.animation.org and select "Women in Animation."

Yahooligans! Art Soup
For girls interested in the visual, performing, and literary arts, Yahooligans! Art Soup offers hours of exploration, with links to museums and performing arts groups around the world, including sites where young artists can exhibit their work on-line. Take a look at www.yahoo.com and follow the links to the Yahooligans! directory.

SPORTS AND PHYSICAL ACTIVITIES

Books, Web sites, and organizations abound to encourage your daughter to be physically active, whether in competitive sports or noncompetitive recreational activities.

BOOKS

There are lots of great books about specific women and girl athletes, but the books below are more general. To track down good books for girls interested in specific sports and players, check out the Just Sports for Women Web site, which features a frequently updated list, Top 10 Books.

Athletes: Dynamic Modern Women (Laurie Lindop, 21st Century Books, 1996, 128 pp., $21.00).
Ten women athletes are profiled in this short volume that gives girls a picture of these women's lives as well as their athletic accomplishments. Women from a wide variety of sports are featured, from speed skater Bonnie Blair and swimmer Diana Nyad to tennis star Monica Seles, ice skater Kristi Yamaguchi, and gymnast Kim Zmeskal.

A Sporting Chance: Sports and Gender (Andy Steiner, Lerner Publications, 1995, 96 pp., $22.00)
Full of role models and inspiration, this book examines the benefits of participation in sports, the variety of sports open to women (and the obstacles that still limit participation), and key historical events that have turned the tide in favor of more equitable practices. Includes photos and a bibliography.

The Quiet Storm: A Celebration of Women in Sport (Alexandra Powe Allred and Michelle Powe, Masters Press, 1998, 256 pp., $15.00).

More than 100 athletes contributed their ideas about women in sports to this book. While celebrating their participation, the authors acknowledge the ongoing challenges and obstacles girls and women still face as athletes. Each contributor discusses her sport and how it has affected other areas of her life, like career, family, and friendship.

Raising Our Athletic Daughters: How Sports Can Build Self-Esteem and Save Girls' Lives (Gil Reavil and Jean Zimmerman, Doubleday, 1998, 320 pp., $23.95).

This book is based on the authors' conversations with girls and young women (and their parents) across the country who have participated in sports and experienced firsthand the benefits they've derived. Increased self-esteem and independence, improved leadership skills, reduced incidence of drug use and pregnancy, and higher educational aspirations are just a few of the benefits described. These personal accounts explore how sports can make such a significant difference in girls' lives and will inspire any parent to encourage her daughter's athletic abilities. Included is information about how parents can have a positive influence, as well a listing of useful books and organizations.

MAGAZINES

Sports Illustrated for Kids

Sports Illustrated for Kids is not just for girls, but it's full of great female role models for pre-teen and young adolescent girls interested in sports. A lively magazine, it includes fun monthly features like the sports calendar, a kids' art gallery, and pull-out sports cards, it's full of great female role models. And the Web site is an adventure for any girl who's interested in sports and athletes.

For more information, contact:

Sports Illustrated for Kids
P.O. Box 830609
Birmingham, AL 35283
(800) 992-0196
www.sikids.com

For information about camps in your area, check the local newspaper in late spring when camps begin advertising for the summer. Also, check www.femina.com, where you can link to information about girls' camps around the country, and visit www.kidscamps.com to locate girls' camps in your area where your daughter can make new friends while enjoying physical challenges.

Kroka Expeditions
Kroka Expeditions offers wilderness experiences for children and adults including a five-day Coming of Age for Young Women for girls twelve to fifteen years old. This special expedition is a celebration of being a young woman that includes physical challenges, game-playing, basketry, and other fun activities. For more information, contact:

> Kroka Expeditions
> RR 2 Box 1218
> Putney, VT 05346
> (802) 387-5397
> kroka@together.net

North Waters Wilderness Program
This outdoor school offers a canoe program for girls eleven to fourteen called Northern Lights, which encourages girls to connect to their true self through weaving, storytelling, creative arts, personal challenge, and ritual.

> For more information, contact:
> Northwaters Wilderness Programs
> P.O. Box 477
> St. Peters, PA 19470
> (610) 469-4661
> www.northwaters.com

Outward Bound
Outward Bound has been offering high-quality outdoor adventures for children and adults since 1961. Over 450,000 people have participated in their programs, which include special courses for teen-

agers designed to teach self-reliance and self-confidence along with the outdoor skills required for each expedition. From whitewater rafting to rock climbing and dog sledding, the programs teach environmental stewardship along with physical, interpersonal, and self-reliance skills.

For more information contact:
Outward Bound National Office
Route 9D
R2 Box 280
Garrison, NY 10524
(888) 882-6863 or (914) 424-4000
www.outwardbound.org

Woodswomen
Woodswomen specializes in outdoor adventures for women of all ages in the United States, Europe, and other spots around the world. Included in the lineup of adventures is a Women and Kids program. While not designed just for girls, a Women and Kids trip can be a great way to share a safe outdoor experience with your daughter. The brochure includes information about how to choose an appropriate expedition.

For more information, contact:
Woodswomen Inc.
25 West Diamond Lake Road
Minneapolis, MN 55419
(800) 279-0555

ORGANIZATIONS AND WEB SITES

CNN Women's Sports Web Site
This site keeps everyone who is interested up to date on the latest scores and events in women's sports. It includes short features on winning teams and athletes, with photos and links to the full feature story. Links to a list of older stories are also included. Take a look at www.CNNSI.com/womens.

Just Sports for Women
This Web site is fun to visit for any girl interested in sports and physical fitness. It's got scores and updates on all the latest women's teams, chat rooms, and Ask an Expert spot where girls can get answers

about exercise, diet, fitness, and other related topics. Profiles and activities of women athletes are featured, including some off-beat sports like adventure racing. Its Services section includes a list of the top ten books on female athletes, an on-line store, and links to other related sites. Check it out at www.justwomen.com.

The National Association for Girls and Women in Sport (NAGWS)
NAGWS has been championing sports equity for women and girls since 1899 and is involved in a variety of activities to accomplish that goal, from influencing public policy and educating parents and teachers to sponsoring special activities and events. Each year the association co-sponsors National Girls and Women in Sport Day, with activities across the country to educate the public and provide opportunities for participation in lots of different sports events. The association's Web site is also fun to visit, with lots of links to women's professional teams and organizations like the Women's National Basketball Association.

For more information, contact:
National Association for Girls and Women in Sport
1900 Association Drive
Reston, VA 20191-1599
(800) 213-7193
www.aahperd.org/nagws

Nike Web Site for Girls
As part of its Play Like a Girl campaign, Nike sponsors this Web site where girls can get in-depth reports on women athletes and teams. These reports, which follow the subject(s) for a day or two, give girls an insider's view of what being a professional athlete is like, from eating and working out to practicing and working with a coach. Girls can join an on-line team that features girls from around the world who write a short description of the sports they're involved in, along with their best and worst sports moments. Visit the site at www.nike.com/girls.

The Women's Sports Foundation
This foundation works to promote women's and girls' lifelong participation in sports and fitness by improving access to organized

sports for girls, sponsoring a speakers' bureau and educational events, offering internships, and funding special activities and athletes through its grant program. For girls who are interested in sports, or if you want to encourage a reluctant daughter, the foundation has a Junior Athlete or Family Membership, which includes a quarterly newsletter in which champion athletes share their ideas about the benefits of sports, along with other articles on self-esteem, fitness, nutrition, and other issues of interest to girls.

For more information, contact:

The Women's Sports Foundation
Eisenhower Park
East Meadow, NY 11554
(800) 227-3988
www.lifetimetv.com/WoSport

The Tucker Center for Research on Girls & Women in Sports

The center is an interdisciplinary research facility working to increase support for, and awareness of, the importance of physical activity in the lives of girls and women. Sports research internships, athletic scholarships, and publications and reports on a variety of issues are available. *Physical Activity & Sport in the Lives of Girls,* an eighty-three-page report, is a compilation of research in the field that anyone with an athletic daughter or an interest in encouraging a daughter's sports participation will find fascinating reading.

For more information, contact:

The Tucker Center for Research on
    Girls & Women in Sports
1900 University Ave. SE
203 Cooke Hall
Minneapolis, MN 55455
(612) 625-7327

STAYING SAFE AND IN CONTROL

The resources included here will help girls feel strong and in control and act intelligently in relation to risks like smoking, alcohol, and sex. For more information on resources to support girls, check out Girls Incorporated and the Girl Scouts (in the "National Organizations" resource listings on page 174) which offer programs around the country on these topics.

Books

Dating Violence: Young Women in Danger (Edited by Barrie Levy, Seal Press, 1998, 324 pp., $18.95).
This book examines the growing incidence of date rape, abuse, and violence and provides insight into why it occurs and what can be done to prevent it. First-person narratives from teens and parents provide a context for the discussions of causes and solutions. Included are descriptions of successful community and school-based programs to educate teens in prevention, as well as to help teens already involved. (Levy is the author of *What Parents Need to Know About Dating Violence*, published in 1995 by Seal Press. Less recent than *Dating Violence*, it still offers excellent information and advice. And for girls who may be involved in abusive relationships, Levy is also the author of *In Love and in Danger: A Teen's Guide to Breaking Free of Abusive Relationships*, published by Seal Press.)

Drug and Alcohol Abuse: The Authoritative Guide for Parents, Teachers, and Counselors (H. Thomas Milhorn, Plenum Press, 1994, 395 pp., $27.95).
Written by an expert on adolescent drug abuse, this book is a good resource for researching drugs and their effects on your daughter. Information on the effects of drugs is complemented by information about why teens become involved with drugs, how to identify drug use, and special problems faced by teenage female drug users.

The Get Prepared Library of Violence Prevention for Young Women (Donna Chaiet, Rosen Publishing Group, 1995, $16.95 to $23.75).
This series of books helps girls stay safe in lots of situations by providing practical tips and suggestions. The series includes titles like *Staying Safe on Dates, Staying Safe on the Streets, Staying Safe at Work, Staying Safe While Traveling*, and others.

It's a Girl Thing: How to Stay Healthy, Safe and in Charge (Mavis Jukes, Knopf, 1997, 207 pp., $5.99).
Laced with stories from her own teen years, the author gives frank

advice for pre-teen and early-teen girls on everything from how to buy a bra to more serious topics, like abusive behavior, HIV, harassment, rape, peer pressure, and sexuality. Her frank, matter-of-fact, and sympathetic style will help girls accept the changes they are going through, while being smart about the risks that come with growing up.

Girl Power: Making Choices and Taking Control (Patty Ellis, Momentum Books, 1994, 198 pp., $9.95).
A self-help guide that stresses action and personal responsibility as keys to feeling confident and in control, this book provides practical advice on topics like peer pressure, abusive situations, substance abuse, and media pressure to conform to an idealized image of women.

The Rights of Women and Girls (Kary Moss and Norman Dorsen, Puffin, 1998, 128 pp., $9.99).
Developed by the American Civil Liberties Union, this book explains what harassment and discrimination are, provides historical information about women's status in society and how women's rights evolved, and discusses court cases that contributed to those rights. Information about what legal rights girls and women have is included, along with ideas about how to handle discrimination and harassment when they do occur. An extensive resource list of useful books and organizations is also included.

Sexual Harassment: A Question of Power (Joann Bren Guernsey, Lerner Publications, 1995, 96 pp., $19.95).
Through real-world examples like the Tailhook scandal, this book helps girls understand what harassment is—in the workplace, in daily life, and at school. Historical and legal perspectives are presented, along with information about how to prevent harassment and what recourse victims have. Diverse points of view are presented, and a discussion of male victims of harassment is included. This book offers a good jumping-off point for discussions with teen girls.

Taking Charge of My Mind and Body: A Girls' Guide to Outsmarting Alcohol, Drugs, Smoking and Eating Problems (Gladys Folkers and Jeanne Engelmann, Free Spirit Publishing, 1997, 208 pp., $13.95).

A reader-friendly approach to helping girls avoid getting involved in self-destructive behaviors that can last a lifetime, this book looks at the issues from a girl's point of view. Specific things to say and do when confronted with opportunities to drink, smoke, or engage in other destructive behaviors are included. Also included is a listing of Web sites, hot lines, and organizations where girls can find useful information or get help.

Venus in Blue Jeans: Why Mothers and Daughters Need to Talk about Sex (Nathalie Bartle and Susan Lieberman, Houghton Mifflin, 1998, 252 pp., $24.00).
Venus in Blue Jeans offers guidance to mothers who want to speak honestly with their daughters about sex without encouraging sexual activity. Interviews with mothers and daughters—and quotes from them—strengthen the open approach to the subject advocated by the authors. Filled with practical suggestions, mothers (and fathers) can use this book to understand adolescent girls' sexuality, evaluate how much their daughters understand, develop strategies for initiating open talks, and create a context for discussions that place sex in the larger context of meaningful relationships.

ORGANIZATIONS, PROGRAMS, AND WEB SITES

Advocates for Youth
Advocates for Youth's mission is to help young people make informed, responsible decisions about their sexuality and reproductive health. The organization provides educational programs and publications on a wide range of topics, from AIDS to pregnancy prevention. Included in its materials is a series of pamphlets written by teens for teens on preventing date rape and sexually transmitted diseases, and on other topics of interest to teens. Parents can order publications on-line and teens can visit the Teen Scene Information page, which offers information, chat opportunities, and links to related sites.

For more information, contact:
Advocates for Youth
1025 Vermont Ave., NW
Suite 200
Washington, DC 20005
(202) 347-5700
www.advocatesforyouth.org

Family Education Network
The Family Education Network offers parents lots of good information about how to help teenagers grow up smart and safe. Diverse topics from education and family to friends and health are covered, with a panel of experts who respond to on-line questions. While safety topics are by no means the only ones covered, parents and teens looking for help in dealing with school violence, drug use, and on-line safety will find lots of good information and resources. Take a look at www.familyeducation.com.

Girl Power (U.S. Department of Health and Human Services)
As part of its Girl Power campaign designed to encourage girls to make the most of their lives, the Department of Health and Human Services has developed a drug-prevention program targeted to girls. A call to the 800 number lets you order a packet of information, including a lively Girl Power diary, bookmarks, and stickers. Also check out the Web site, where you can find information about the Girl Power campaign and on-line information about drugs and their effects on the body.

For more information, contact:
> U.S. Department of Health and Human Services
> The National Clearinghouse for Alcohol and Drug
>   Information
> P.O. Box 2345
> Rockville, MD 20847
> Girl Power Campaign
> (800) 729-6686
> www.health.org

Model Mugging Program
Model Mugging teaches a specialized form of self-defense that has been endorsed by law-enforcement officials, hospitals, and rape-crisis centers as the most effective self-defense training available for women. Developers of the program see fighting as a last resort but recognize that women must be prepared to defend themselves against violent attacks and sexual assaults. Deterrence and techniques for stopping an attack quickly are emphasized, and women and girls learn to function effectively in a state of fear. A special program for

adolescent girls, TeenPower, uses date/acquaintance rape scenarios as part of its training. Model Mugging programs are offered in a number of states around the country. For information about locations, call 800-345-KICK or log on to the Bay Area Model Mugging Web site (www.bamm.org), where you'll find a list of Model Mugging sites around the country, as well as lots of information about their programs.

National Center for Tobacco-Free Kids

Despite the well-known health risks of smoking and a decline in smoking overall in recent decades, teens and young adults have started smoking again in unprecedented numbers. And it's no wonder. It's commonplace now to see teen idols smoking in movies, and years of "cool" ad campaigns have glamorized smoking. The center's national campaign is working to reverse the trend. Kids and parents can participate in this campaign through educational activities and an annual anti-smoking event called (what else?) Kick Butt Day. Girls can log on to the Web site to get good information about the health effects of smoking and hear what celebrity teens have to say about staying away from this self-destructive addiction.

For more information, contact:

National Center for Tobacco-Free Kids
1707 L Street NW
Suite 800
Washington, DC 20036
(800) 284-KIDS
www.tobaccofreekids.org

Planned Parenthood

This national organization with centers across the country provides education, low-cost exams, and other resources for young people and adults to help them make safe, intelligent reproductive and sexuality choices. In addition to looking into resources at a clinic in your area, visit their Web site alone or with your daughter. You'll both find helpful information about reproductive and sexuality issues. Parents will find tips on how to talk with teens about sex, while girls will find information about dating, relationships, staying healthy, sexually transmitted diseases, and other topics. Girls can also take an on-line Sex IQ test to see how smart they are about sexuality, staying safe, and making good choices.

For more information, contact:

> Planned Parenthood Federation of America
> 810 7th Ave.
> New York, NY 10019
> (212) 541-7800
> (800) 230-PLAN (connects caller to the closest Planned
>   Parenthood center)
> www.plannedparenthood.org

Rape Abuse & Incest National Network (RAINN)

The RAINN network offers a national hot line and counseling for victims of sexual abuse. The hot line operates twenty-four hours a day, connecting callers to the closest rape-crisis center in their area. All callers receive confidential counseling and support. For statistics on rape and assault, visit the Web site, where you'll find lots of information to discuss with your daughter.

For more information, contact:

> Rape Abuse & Incest National Network (RAINN)
> 635-B Pennsylvania Ave. SE
> Washington, DC 20003
> (800) 656-HOPE

Sexuality Information and Education Council of the U.S. (SIECUS)

SIECUS is a nonprofit organization involved in program development and educational and public-policy efforts to advocate for the right to make responsible sexual choices. The organization and its Web site are gold mines of information for parents who want to help their children develop healthy attitudes toward sexuality, resist peer pressure, prevent sexually transmitted diseases, and avoid sexual violence or exploitation. They publish their own materials and maintain a reading list of books for parents and kids on topics as diverse and useful as how to talk about sex, sexual development, pregnancy prevention, sexual abuse, and more. The Web site includes links to other related organizations.

For more information, contact:

Sexuality Information and Education Council of the U.S.
   (SIECUS)
130 West 42nd St.
Suite 350
New York, NY 10036
(212) 819-9770
www.siecus.org

APPENDIX/THE SURVEY

Here are the questions included in the survey for successful teens, whose answers and suggestions have been used throughout this book.

Please provide specific examples of experiences and activities that helped you in each of the areas addressed by the questions below. The suggestions given in some questions are included to spark your creativity and not to influence your ideas. I'm looking for your uniqueness and special insights. . . .

QUESTION 1

Please describe one family activity you participated in (regularly or infrequently) during your growing up years that contributed to helping you feel good about yourself. Why do you think this activity contributed to your self-esteem? If you did not grow up in a traditional nuclear family, or if you were most influenced by a family-like group or individual who served as a family or parental surrogate (perhaps a friend's family with whom you spent a lot of time), please use an example from this relationship.

QUESTION 2

If there were one thing you would tell every mother to do for, or with, her daughter before or during adolescence to help build her self-confidence, what would it be and why? If you did not have a close relationship with your mother or if you did not know your mother, what one piece of advice would you give women who want to make a positive difference in girls' lives?

QUESTION 3

If there were one thing you would tell every father to do for, or with, her daughter before or during adolescence to help build her self-confidence, what would it be and why? If you did not have a close relationship with your father or if you did not know your father, what one piece of advice would you give men who want to make a positive difference in girls' lives?

QUESTION 4

The concept of "Girl Power" is becoming popular. Lots of people are saying sugar and spice aren't nice, that girls should speak out, play hard, stand up for themselves, and go after their dreams. Please describe an experience or activity that helped you do any of the things just mentioned, and explain why you think it did. (Examples might include attending all-girl events, joining an organization, taking a particular class, volunteering, running a business, or working for a cause.)

QUESTION 5

Around adolescence many girls stop participating in activities they enjoy and don't get involved in new ones. Many girls who successfully navigated adolescence say they stayed involved in lots of activities and tried new ones that were challenging and required taking some personal risk (like a physical challenge or doing something that made other people notice them). If this is true for you, describe an important activity that contributed to your confidence and self-esteem. Remember to include information about any resources that helped you in that activity.

QUESTION 6

For many girls, adolescence is synonymous with dieting and dissatisfaction with their bodies. Girls who escape the dangerous aspects of this common pattern say things like participating in sports, or living in a family where the unrealistic image of women in the media was discussed, helped them accept and feel good about their bodies. Describe one thing (an activity, experience, or relationship) that has helped you maintain a healthy body image. Remember to include information about any resources that were helpful.

QUESTION 7

Girls get many mixed messages about what they can be and do. They get the message they can become superwomen and do it all at the same time they realize boys might like them better if they play dumb. These kinds of mixed messages can affect the activities girls participate in and the dreams they have for their futures. Describe an activity, experience, or relationship (for example, an internship, job, class, summer businesses, etc.) that helped you develop a dream and work toward it.

QUESTION 8

Many women find out too late that having economic control of their lives is a key part of feeling good about themselves and having the resources to create the lives they want. Please briefly describe your attitudes toward money and money management and describe one activity that helped you understand and manage money. Or, if you did not learn money-management skills in pre-adolescence or adolescence, what kinds of experiences do you wish you had had during that period?

QUESTION 9

Opportunities to participate in experiences that help build self-esteem and confidence can be affected by your economic, racial, ethnic, or religious background. Special conditions, such as a physical handicap, may also play a part in access to opportunities and experiences. If these issues, or any others you would like to specify, have affected you, please describe an activity or experience that has helped or hindered your ability to develop fully. (This is a very complex issue; please feel free to go beyond a discussion of activities and experiences if you have time.)

QUESTION 10

What top five recommendations would you give adults who want to help girls grow up smart, strong, and confident? (You can use ideas from your other answers.) To come up with these top five, you might think about things (like resources, relationships, activities, etc.) you believe are often missing for girls.

Index

206